Adoption – Changing One's Stars
The Search for Blue Eyes

Solomon L. Stamm

Copyright © 2016 by Solomon L. Stamm

Adoption – Changing One's Stars
The Search for Blue Eyes
by Solomon L. Stamm

Printed in the United States of America

ISBN–13: 978-1530747375
ISBN–10: 1530747376

All rights reserved solely of the author. The author guarantees all contents are original and do not infringe upon the legal rights of any other person or work. No part of this publication may be reproduced or transmitted in any form or by any means without written permission of the author. The views expressed in this book are not necessarily those of the publisher.

To purchase additional copies of this book, visit Amazon.com

Acknowledgements

Thank you to the following individuals who without their contributions and support this book would not have been written.

Melissa Stamm Falkowski – editor, layout, and book design

Phyllis and Ron Dolislager – advisors and mentors

Ma'ayan Rosensweig Rattner – cover design

My Snyder siblings – Ruth, Leroy, Amos, and Delores for answering all my many questions

Snyder nieces and nephews who contributed their memories – MaryAnna, Wendy, Nancy, Vicki, Tracy, Cathy, Sandy, Ellen, Lisa, Mike, and Sherry

A special thanks to my brother, Warren Stamm, for understanding why I needed to write this book, and for his willingness to allow me to share my story, which is obviously intertwined with his.

Dedication

To the Women in My Life:

Elizabeth Carver Snyder, my birth mother
Edith Gardner Stamm, my adopted mother
Joy Hauser Stamm, my wife

I was once told that on the day you are born, the day you are to die is written in the Book of Life. And I suppose that life itself is nothing more than a series of chances and/or decisions made that move us to that fateful end.

So far I've lived a very good life. Some, including myself, would say, a charmed life. For that I owe it all to two special mothers. Although they didn't know each other, together they MADE MY LIFE. I dedicate this book to them – I truly love you both.

The third woman in my life is, of course, my life partner and wife, Joy. She has supported me, encouraged me, and loved me. She is my rock, and the love of my life. I love you, Dear.

Preface

Adoption...that word. While it has a single definition, it also has many different meanings, and it covers a spectrum of emotions.

For those with closed adoptions, some may search for their birth family from the time they find out that they were adopted. Others, so as not to upset their adoptive parents, let it simmer awhile until they are of legal age to begin their search. Still others have no desire to search. They're comfortable in their own lives, until some life-changing event sends them out on their search. I fall into the last category.

For me it was "blue eyes" that sent me out on my search. While I had tried half-heartedly ten years before – one letter to a state agency, and it was done – this time was different. My second grandson was born with blue eyes, and no one in the family had blue eyes. After some genealogy research, it all pointed back to me as the source of his blue eyes.

All my life I knew I was adopted, and I was comfortable with it and with my life. I never wanted to search. As my son would say, "I'm risk adverse." I would say, "You never know what you might turn up."

I've heard horror stories of adoptees being rebuffed by their mothers, who had gone on to marry and have families. I also heard happy ending stories like the twin sisters who recently found each other by happen stance on YouTube videos, not knowing the other even existed.

I was quite apprehensive, but off we went. I say "we," as my wife Joy, who is truly my partner in everything I do, was right by my side to help and encourage me.

What I uncovered has opened my world in a way that I never could have imagined. That said, for me at age 56, the time was right for searching. Even in finding this new world that I didn't know existed, there is nothing I would have changed about my past.

Life can only be understood backwards, but it must be lived forwards – Kierkegaard

Introduction

I never thought about writing a book. In fact, the only experience I have in writing is with business correspondence or college papers in the very distant past. Then on January 14, 2013, I received a response to a letter I sent to the State of Florida asking for non-identifying information about my adoption. The response, from what I understand to be the norm, was unusually detailed, and it changed my life's beliefs...and me...forever.

After reading the letter and sharing the information in it with family, friends and co-workers, they always showed significant interest and almost always ended the conversation with, "that should be a movie" and "thanks for sharing." At that point I had a fleeting thought of maybe writing down my life's story, but it was just that, a fleeting thought–until a chance meeting with an author while on vacation.

Joy and I were on a Transatlantic cruise, and on the second night we were randomly paired with two other couples for dinner, Phyllis and Ron Dolislager and a British couple, Victor and Roseanne Smith. What threw us together that night was pure chance. While we ate, we talked about this and that, and it was easy conversation throughout dinner. As we were finishing up, Phyllis told us that she was the author of a number of books including her memoirs. She gave us a copy of one of the books.

It was at that point that the fleeting thought of writing my story welled up in me, and I said, "Boy do I have a story for you," but added, "it's a long one." They all wanted to hear it, so off I went. Using one of my adopted mother's famous sayings, "to make a long story short" (and they never were), we talked for another hour or so, and we closed the dining room, as we were the last to leave.

It was at that point that I knew I really had to write this book telling my story of adoption and my family's story. Phyllis invited me to come by her cabin the next day saying that she would help me get started. Little did I know she would prepare notes for me and give me "homework" assignments. Phyllis taught at Nova Southeastern University in Davie, Florida, thus the homework assignments.

On sea days I wrote and turned in "my assignments." This helped to solidify my feeling and determination to write this book.

Victor and Roseanne also helped push me along. We dined again with them a couple of nights after our first encounter. Victor was so intrigued by the story, he asked me to keep him posted on my progress. He gave me his business card and said they'd be back in South Florida in November, and he wanted us to get together.

It seems that fate, or as some would say, "all the stars were in alignment" for this book to come to be. I remember a movie I once saw with Heath Ledger called, "A Knight's Tale." He was a Thatcher's son, who left his family as his father gave him up, so Ledger could serve as a knight's squire, in the hopes he could change his stars. He did, and he became a knight.

This is truly the story of my life, as my birth mother gave me up for adoption, allowing me to "change MY stars."

Contents

Part 1 – Life on the Beach

Garden Avenue 1
Lenny and Edith 5
Meridian Avenue 17
Relatives Visit 25
Miami Beach Fun in the Sun 29
Pool Boys 33
Stoner Days 39
A Philadelphia Connection 43
Out From the Cold 51

Part 2 – Life, No Longer Just Self

Life Partner 53
Married with Children 59
Random Thoughts 71
Work–Successes, Disappointments, and Dead Bodies 77
Globetrotters 89

Part 3 – The Search, The Letter, The Crazy Week

Mindset on Searching for My Birth Family 97
The Letter – January 14, 2013 101
A Crazy Week Unfolds 107
Adoption and my Brother Warren 115

Part 4 – Parallel Universes Collide

Birth Parents – Elizabeth and Orville 121
The First Meeting – February 2013 125
Individual Sessions with Living Siblings 131
Surviving Siblings 135
Siblings that Have Passed 163

Part 5 – Discovering Ancestry

English and Dutch 183
Historical Connections–Carver and Doan in my Blood 185

Part 6 – The Unmasking Of Me

Final Accounting 191

Part 7 – Epilogue

In Memory of Ruth 197

Part 8 – Reference To Help With Adoption Search

Contacts 199

Part 9 – Appendix

Lists 201

Life on the Beach

Garden Avenue

In the early 1950's, Miami Beach was a vacation spot. It was the "in" place to be with the likes of Arthur Godfrey, the "Rat Pack," and lots of other movie stars. With the weather and the surf, my adopted parents decided that that's where they wanted to be.

They vacationed there for several years, but it would be several more years before they actually moved to Florida. That came in late 1953, and was spurred by the passing of my paternal grandfather. It was at that point that my father, a practicing optometrist and part-time fight promoter, sold his practice and their property in Philadelphia and moved south. The rest of their family never left, but they would visit us from time to time.

Garden Avenue, Miami Beach circa 1957.
Dad, Me and Mom.

Not only did my parents move, but my father also changed his line of work at 33 years old, never to be an optometrist again. He hated being cooped up in an office. More about his newly-chosen profession later, let's just say it was 180 degrees from what he was doing in Philadelphia.

They rented this little house near St. Patrick's Church on Garden Avenue in Miami Beach. The next several years their circle of friends grew, and they decided to stay in Florida. They also decided it was time for a family, and they knew, due to a medical issue, they would have to adopt. One of their closest friends back in Philadelphia was Dr. David Silverman. It was Dr. Silverman who was able to find them a baby to adopt and made all the arrangements.

Me circa 1957, shortly after my parents' return to Miami Beach from Philadelphia

I was born on October 22, 1956 in Philadelphia Osteopathic Hospital. My parents flew up from Miami Beach to pick me up. They never met my birth mother while picking me up, which was the norm back in the 1950s. Instead, I was handed to my adopted parents, and off we went to a relative's house for a party in my honor. We didn't stay long in Philadelphia as life on "the beach" awaited.

Before we left Philadelphia, I was named. In the Jewish religion, names are chosen to honor and remember those who have passed on. While it was not necessary to use the same English name of the deceased, it was customary to use the first letter of the person's English name. For the Hebrew name it was customary to use the exact Hebrew name of the one you are honoring. I was named Solomon Louis. Solomon was for my father's father, and Louis was for my father's brother, both of whom had passed away a few years earlier. The names were exact in English as in Hebrew. My

Life on the Beach

Life on the beach was all about sun and the surf. Dad and me at the Algiers Hotel cabana

Hebrew name is Sholmo Levy, son of Moshe Levy.

When we arrived in Miami Beach, it was to the rented house on Garden Avenue, and that is where my earliest memories were formed. I remember relatives visiting and staying for quite a while. I was happy and played with a swing set in the backyard and a replica fire engine peddle car. We went to the beach frequently and had a cabana at the Algiers Hotel. Little did I know that the Algiers Hotel would play a role in my life once again as a teenager.

I learned to swim at that hotel, as well as jump and dive from the high diving board at a very young age. I also met Betty Chesky there. Betty was my mother's closest friend, and she was always a part of my life. Betty had three sons, with the middle one, David, the same age as me. We became good friends as we went through school together. Several years later we ended up calling him Dukie, after Duke Ellington, once he learned to play the piano. He was and is that good.

Mom and me at the pool

When I was three and a half, my parents had another baby. Well "had" is probably the wrong term, as they adopted again. This time the baby was born in Miami. The adoption was arranged through our family pediatrician, who oddly enough was connected with David Silverman, who had delivered me. So it was 1960, and I now had a baby brother named Warren. I remember going with my parents to a tiny hospital in Miami to pick him up, a memory that would serve me well later in life.

The Garden Avenue house was small, and I had to share a room with the baby. As I recall I was not so keen on that idea, nor the results. We soon outgrew that house. My mom began to search for a bigger house to buy, much to the chagrin of my father. It didn't take her long, and she didn't search far, as she found a house on Meridian Avenue, which was right around the corner, and on the same block as the one we were renting.

Today the house on Garden Avenue is a part of St. Patrick's Church.

Front row from left: Betty, Dukie, Me, Norman

Me, age 8, 1964

Lenny And Edith

Before I move any further with my life, I should give some background on my adopted parents, Lenny and Edith Stamm.

Lenny and Edith met in Atlantic City in 1940. From what my mother's sister, Rose, tells me, there were about a dozen guys trying to get a date with my mom. It was a summer day on the beach, and Lenny stepped forward and asked her out. One of the other guys said, "Hey buddy, get in line," but Lenny being Lenny had no part of that conversation and got the date.

Edith's family was poor in comparison to the other Stamm sibling spouses. That didn't matter to Lenny, and he chased after her. She was 15 years old and was studying at a vocational high school to be a beautician. She also worked at a local drug store part-time, and Lenny, who was 19, would wait for her in his car on Friday nights to take her out and then home.

They dated for a few years, and Lenny went to serve in WWII, serving primarily in France.

Lenny off to serve as an optometrist in a hospital in France

They were married on October 20, 1945, in Philadelphia. She was 20 years old, and he was 24. They got married quickly upon his return from the war as his mother was very sick, and they didn't know if she would even make it until their wedding. Originally, they planned to get married in the Rabbi's study, but at the last minute a dinner was arranged since his mother was well enough to attend. It was a small ceremony followed by a dinner. She wore

Lenny and Edith wedding picture
October 20, 1946

no wedding dress, but looked absolutely stunning. Thus began a happy union of Lenny and Edith.

Edith was the fourth out of five children. She had one brother and three sisters. Like a lot of others, she lied about her age so she could work at an early age. In Philadelphia she worked for Bonwitt Teller and for Wannamaker's. Edith was always into fashion.

From seeing pictures and from others' accounts of her, people said she looked like Ava Gardner. I could see the resemblance. She always dressed well and had her hair done. She was one of those ladies, who went to the beauty parlor every Saturday and got her hair washed and set for the week. It always looked perfect.

Edith had a tubal pregnancy a number of years before I was adopted. Her sister Rose, recounted that she was lucky to have survived, as she almost bled to death. Years went by, and they were not able to have children, so they adopted.

She was for the most part a homemaker. That said, she did work part-time in a boutique on Miami Beach, and her customers loved her and came back repeatedly. She could put an outfit together. I think she did it for two reasons: one to have something to do that gave her a little of her own spending money, and two, to get away from my father for a while.

When she wasn't working, she was shopping, usually with her best friend Betty. They would shop for hours at Bloomingdales,

Macy's, Burdines, and Jordan Marsh. They hit them all. At the end of the day, there was very little they bought, as she didn't have much to spend. The allure was just being out with her friend. I also must say, she did love a good bargain.

Edith and Betty, best friends for 65 years

She also played cards, gin rummy, once a week with a different set of friends. It was usually a weeknight, and it went on for several hours with only a couple dollars changing hands at the end of the night.

We went out to eat so often that I really don't remember her cooking very much. What I do remember is her brisket, rice and gravy being the best ever. Joy now makes it for me, using her recipe. The other thing she did well was to bake. One recipe in particular Joy carries on today, Mandel Bread. It's like a Jewish type of biscotti. When Joy makes it, it starts to disappear before it even cools.

My brother and I owe everything to our mother. As you'll see later on in this chapter, my father was a different type of person, and without my mom balancing him a bit, there is no telling how we would have ended up. She gave us encouragement throughout the years, pushed us to finish school, and even fought with our dad to allow us to go to college.

She used to enjoy the gambling junkets to Atlantic City and Vegas, but especially Atlantic City. It gave her the opportunity to see her family. It also allowed her the freedom to play Blackjack by herself, without my father, giving her some time away from him.

When my father had a heart attack in 1994, she said to me, "My life is over." Well, it wasn't, but from then on her away time was minimal. She still managed to get away with Betty every chance she could.

In 2000, my brother took a job in Las Vegas, and my father decided he would sell the house and move out there with my brother. My mother did not want to go, but she had no choice. What he said was law, so he sold the house and off to Vegas they went. They lived well out in Vegas, going to the casinos multiple times a week. With my brother's family there, they went out to dinner with them almost every night of the week.

From time to time, she would ditch him and fly back to Miami Beach to meet up with Betty for a week, hanging out and shopping. Vegas lasted four years, until my father passed away. She stayed out there alone for another six months before returning to Miami.

We bought her a place at Quayside Terrace, in the same building as Betty, and they had a great two-year run before Alzheimer's kicked in. Right before my father died, I promised him that I would take care of her, and for the past twelve years that is exactly what I have done. Never wanting to be institutionalized, since she knew her mother had the same disease, I put her in a small private house near to us where she has been well cared for. I visit her every weekend and sit with her. There is no conversation, as she does not recognize me at this point. She is content and lives in her own little world, talking to herself and to an imaginary Betty.

****

Lenny was a complex person. In spite of his faults, he loved and provided for his family. Saying that is somewhat cleansing for me. It helps to clear the air before I attempt to write about him. It's a statement about him at the highest level–what's coming next will be Lenny exposed, piece by piece.

Lenny lived life with a much different philosophy than me. His catch phrase was, "Do to others, before they do to you." That's probably why we never got along. Sure I loved him, he was my father.

Lenny's actual name was not Lenny, but Morris. Lenny was his middle name, and while I know a lot of people go by their middle name, it was the start of things about Lenny that weren't what they appeared to be. He was a Doctor of Optometry, but that's not what he did for a living. He was a loving husband, but he was the boss. He was a father to my brother and me, but he sometimes verbally abused me for not being "street smart," while he praised my brother. All the while all my brother ever did was feed him whatever he wanted to hear, to stay in his good graces.

What Lenny was...was a survivor. He grew up as the youngest of nine children. He was ten years younger than his closest sibling; some were old enough to be his mother. That is where the similarities between us start and end. His brothers were optometrists, dentists, jewelry makers, and owners of a typical corner store.

Lenny's family home at 2nd & Catherine, South Philadelphia. The name, S. Stamm, is his father, who I am named after

Besides those legitimate businesses, they were also into gambling. There were days from the bleachers at Connie Mack stadium in Philadelphia that they ran "book" and "bet" on every pitch. They also ran "book" from the corner store. Watching and learning from his brothers is where his career as a doctor ended, before it began.

He went to the Philadelphia School of Optometry, and those are the earliest stories I heard about him skirting the system, or as I like to say, "blurring the lines between right and wrong." While becoming an optometrist, he befriended the smartest kid in the class to help him get through the classes and the tests. Now don't get me wrong, Lenny was plenty smart and most likely could have done it on his own, but that just wasn't his style.

So he became an optometrist and practiced while serving in the army during World War II. He served in Europe in hospitals well back from the front. When he came home from the war, he practiced in Philadelphia. As a result of his wheeling and dealing, by the time he gave up the profession in 1953, he owned half a dozen stores surrounding his practice.

That was a significant year. His brother Louie passed away, and then his father one week later, as they say, "from a broken heart that his son Louie died." Those deaths freed him from practicing Optometry, and he sold his practice and the other stores, and my parents moved to Florida.

In addition, he moonlighted as a fight promoter. He sponsored

Lenny and Rocky Marciano, World Heavy Weight Champion from 1952-1956

many fights, along with his friend Jimmy DiPiano. There are old family photographs of the great Rocky Marciano and other fighters that he promoted. In the late 1970's, he was quoted in Sports Illustrated, after his lifelong friend Jimmy DiPiano's son, who went by his mother's maiden name of Rossman, beat Victor Golendez for the Light Heavyweight title of the world. His name was Mike Rossman, "the Jewish bomber." He won that fight in

Optometrist Gets License to Promote Boxing at the Met

Dr. M. L. Stamm to Stage First Show Next Week

Dr. M. L. Stamm, an optometrist living at 5318 Market st., has been granted a license by the State Athletic Commission to promote boxing shows at the Met for the remainder of the indoor season. Dr. Stamm heads a syndicate of sportsmen who rented the Met from owner Jimmy Toppi for five consecutive Thursday nights, beginning March 29, with an option to operate on additional dates if the venture is successful.

The new promoter was granted a license by Commissioner John (Ox) DaGrosa after presenting a receipt from Toppi in the amount of $1,875, representing full rental for the five initial dates, and required bonds.

Jack Puggy, veteran of the fight game as boxer, manager and trainer for the last quarter century, will serve as matchmaker for Dr. Stamm. Puggy's matchmaking experience includes many years as an assistant to Pete Moran under promoter Herman Taylor and also includes the three annual benefit shows for the Deborah Sanatorium.

Puggy's first card, now in the making, will be announced before the end of the week. It is booked for Thursday night of next week.

1950

Boxer Mike Rossman, "The Jewish Bomber." Photo by John Iacono, published in December 18, 1978 Sports Illustrated

Rossman was stretched out on a rumpled bed in an unpretentious Philadelphia hotel room he shared with his younger brother Andy. Jimmy DePiano was hovering nearby. The new champion recalled a conversation with a friend last Sept. 15 in New Orleans. It had occurred a few hours after Rossman had stopped Victor Galindez in the 13th round to win the title. The friend was Dr. Leonard Stan of Miami.

They had met after the fight, and Stan had given Rossman a long, thoughtful look. Then he had said, "You're no longer Mike Rossman."

Startled, Rossman asked him what he meant by that.

"Yesterday you were Mike Rossman," Stan said. "Today and every day after, you belong to the people."

Rossman admitted it had taken him a few days before he was able to under-

Rossman hit his stride after converting himself from a cute counterpuncher into the big banger.

stand what it was that Stan had meant.

"I was in a bar somewhere," he said. "I just wanted a few beers. That's all I drink. But I like one or two sometimes. The people in the bar knew who I was. They were giving me funny looks. I could almost hear the rumor spreading. Well, he's the champion and there he is, juicing it up. I got out of there in a hurry and I haven't been in a bar since.

"I still like a couple of beers now and then. But if I want them, I buy them in a store and I take them home and drink them. Being champion, it's a heavy responsibility. It is to me, anyway. I want to show I can be a champion in public as well as a champion in the ring."

Excerpt from "Meet Their Son, The World Champion" by Pat Putnam. Published in December 18, 1978 Sports Illustrated the New Orleans Superdome as the undercard to a Muhammad Ali, heavyweight title bout.

No one in Florida knew he was an optometrist, and he then began using his "street smarts," that he learned from his older brothers, to make a living. He owned bars. I met the Harlem Globetrotters at one, but most of all he was a bookie and a loan shark, doing anything that he could to make a buck.

As a child, I remember going with him to "make stops" as he called it. What that entailed was going up and down Miami Beach and stopping at hotel after hotel to collect outstanding loans or gambling debts. Some of those debts were paid in cash and some with goods. I found out much later that my first set of golf clubs came from the bellmen's storage room at the Fontainebleu Hotel, stolen and given to my father as payment for a debt.

We would go out to restaurants where the owner or manager owed him money, so dinner was free. The funniest was when we went to The Pub. Even though there were long waits, we never waited more than five minutes. Once the maître' d saw him, he would always call for the Dr. Green party, that's what we were known as. I interpreted that as "Dr. Money."

There was the time I wanted an 8-track player for the car. We went to a Montgomery Ward store, and when we went to pay, the cashier rang up the stock number as the price ($15.98 instead of $125). I was about to say something to correct her, and he looked at me and said, "Shut up." He then proceeded to tell her that he wanted a second one, so she should ring it up, and he'd pull it from the shelf. She did and he did. He then returned the second one the next day for full price, of course, and pocketed the money. This marked another time he was disappointed in my street smarts.

Then there were the gambling junkets. He had the casinos in both Atlantic City and Vegas fooled. They paid for my parents' trips—airfare, room, limos, and meals, as they thought he was a big gambler, or so called "high roller." Instead, he just killed time playing baccarat, and he took markers (credit from the casinos at no interest with repayment in 60 days or so). As he did this, he'd put chips in his pockets, and then he gave them to other people to cash them in. In doing that, the casino always thought he was a big loser. On the contrary, he'd then take their money and invest it in a Certificate of Deposit, and then give them back their own money after he made interest on their money. So let's recap, the casino paid for everything, and he took their money and made money on it. A classic Lenny move.

Flying on a plane was interesting back then. Long before 9/11 and electronic tickets, we had a way to fly unlike many others. Old time travelers will remember tickets used to be typed, and then if you changed flights, a hand-written sticker would be placed over the old flight. Well, Lenny used to write his own tickets, and we'd show up using tickets made out to other people. I hated to fly that way, but again I wasn't "street smart."

I've worked for most of my adult life for the local power company. What's somewhat funny about that is, when I was a kid, Lenny used to steal electricity from them. He'd go out and mess with the meter and come up with a bill month after month for about $50. They never caught him, and he stopped doing it before I went to work for the utility.

The last Lenny story I'm not proud of, but it happened. As I've said, he was a bookie, and as such he sometimes had the law looking for him. While he never got caught, a partner of his was caught, and did time for bookmaking. During that time I was a teen in the 70's, and from time to time I was known to have some marijuana in the house. Well, he got so pissed at me one time when he found some in my room that he came after me physically. I put a chair in his way, and he fell over it, hurting his arm, which was never the same again. As it turns out, the authorities were after him at that point, and if they had raided the house and found my pot, he would have been blamed for it.

So that was my old man–never having a real job, but doing things to keep a roof over our heads and put food on the table–under his terms. Even with all the emotional baggage, in his way he loved us. You may find this strange, but even though we had our differences in philosophy of life, as an adult I'd still call him for "my daily dose of him." Joy finally smartened me up by telling me to just talk about the weather and to stop seeking his approval on things. I WAS always in search of his approval. With that advice, our relationship smoothed out a bit.

One thing I will say is he LOVED his grandchildren, and he never missed an opportunity to see them. When they'd act up at dinner, he was the one to take them out for a walk or just take them, so that we could eat. That said, I would be remiss if I didn't say that his last encounter with my daughter Sarah was not a good one. He had only good intentions and was only looking out for her happiness, but he said the wrong thing at the wrong time, and she never forgave him.

He passed away from congestive heart failure in 2003; he was 82 years old. One chilling fact was that I had spoken to him the night before he passed away. While he was in hospice, he sounded good. The next morning I awoke and told Joy that I had a feeling that he passed away during the night and that if I got a call that morning it would really freak me out. We were out having a quick lunch and running errands, and I got the call from my sister-in-law. I guess even though we had different points of view on life, we were still connected.

Life on the Beach

Lenny and Edith through the years

Meridian Avenue

The house on Meridian Avenue was purchased for $19,500 and became the family house for 38 years. It wasn't a large house by today's standards, but it was nice. It was two stories with three bedrooms upstairs and two baths. Downstairs there was a maid's room with a full bath that was turned into a breakfast room/den. When we first bought the house it needed a lot of repairs. The previous owner was a very old woman, who had let the place run down, both inside and out.

I remember a couple of things specific to the day we moved in. First there was an electric power chair that moved the old woman between the floors. That didn't last long. Once the repairs were made to the house, it was gone. No matter, Warren and I liked sliding down the stairs anyway. The second item I remember is that Betty came over to wish us well in the new house, and I asked her if I could go with her and sleep at her house with Dukie and Norman, her sons. She said it would be bad luck if I slept away the first night at the new house. So although I remember being disappointed, I stayed.

Obviously my parents got the master bedroom, but then since I was the oldest, I got the larger of the two remaining bedrooms. That only lasted a few years, as I realized that my brother actually got the better deal with the small room. That was due to the fact that the large bedroom came with a large closet, which my father took half of, and he came in anytime he wanted to get something. Thus, the room turned into, 'no privacy.' It wasn't long before I figured it out and got my brother to switch with me. It, being the larger room, he jumped on the idea and couldn't figure out why I wanted to switch, until it was too late.

In the sixties we lived through two hurricanes in that house, Donna and Cleo. There was never a thought of leaving the house for some other shelter, even though we were on Miami Beach, an evacuation zone. You see that house was built in 1938 and was poured concrete over CBS block, and it was raised five feet with a crawl space for water to run through underneath. The interior walls were not drywall like today, but rather Dade Pine studs with wire mesh and stucco. That house was going nowhere, and we all knew it.

The two storms we rode out were different, although they did have a common theme, which was—loss of power. This was due to the Beach's electrical system, which was all overhead wiring. In the first, I was still in the large front bedroom with a large palm tree out in front. Two things happened in that storm. The palm tree fell across the street, making it impassable. If the tree would have fallen the other way, it would have landed right on my room. The other was that the streets flooded from the canals overflowing their banks due to the tidal surge. I remember when it receded there were fish in the street.

The second storm was a lot of wind and very little rain. In fact, during the eye of the hurricane we went outside, and a tree in the neighbor's yard across the street had come down. That was actually good for us. We had lost so many balls in that tree that we quickly grabbed up a couple of footballs, a few softballs, and a Frisbee that had been stuck up there for years.

After one of the storms, my father decided he wanted to replace our lawn of weeds with a circular driveway. He got somebody to do it on the cheap, and they left a gap between the sidewalk and the driveway. He decided to create a coral rock wall in that empty space and enlisted me to do it. Little did I know we'd be driving to the Venetian Causeway to steal coral rocks from a wall that was under repair from the hurricane that had just come through. Imagine their surprise when they got to the end and didn't have enough rocks to finish the job!

When there was company over, my parents would get Warren and me to "do a little shtick" from the stairs looking over the living room. We used to sing songs from the Beatles. My mother thought that was so cute. Looking back I could have passed on that whole experience. My parents used to throw a New Year's Eve party every year for at least 50 people. I usually disappeared to my best friend Marc's house to get away from it all.

Marc's mom's name was Ronnie, and he had two sisters, Roseanne and Lois. Ronnie was like a pal to the kids, rather than a mom and made decisions accordingly. That made my parents' blood boil. When I met Marc in preschool, Ronnie was on her second husband, Harold, or so we thought. He was actually number three. There would be many more as the years went on. My parents despised the fact that I would run over there anytime we had a disagreement... and Ronnie would take me in. One time I was over at Marc's, and I played sick and stayed home from school. Ronnie had Marc and me steaming wall paper off in his room. My parents were livid. As a parent now, I can see why.

During our childhood, Warren and I didn't get along too well. Our personalities were very different. I would tell my parents the facts, like it was. He would tell them what they wanted to hear. We got into big fights. There were a ton of marks and dents in the bedroom doors from objects being hurled at each other, with the door being used as a shield. He did get me good once, but not by a flying object. It was a Number 2 lead pencil that stuck in my side. Not to worry, I got him back.

On my 8th birthday, my parents threw a birthday party for me. As the house had no family room, my parents had the bright idea to throw the party in the garage. Opening the garage doors created a breeze through the space, so it wasn't bad. But what I remember most is my brother slamming my hand in the car

My 8th birthday party, right before Warren slams my hand in the car door

door, and me running around the house several times before they could stop me to see how bad it was. I survived.

My parents used to say they had a revolving charge account at the Mt. Sinai emergency room since one of us was always there. I think it was mostly me, not Warren. Several examples of my visits there include:

- Being hit by a car on my bicycle going to Marc's house
- Being hit by a rock right between the eyes while fooling around on a playground with another kid as we used each other as targets (Didn't say I was too smart back then)
- Breaking my ankle playing basketball (Later I ripped the cast off myself, a week before it was supposed to come off, to get ready for a date–again not too smart)
- Breaking my wrist a day after I took the cast off my ankle, while playing basketball again (Once more, not too smart)

Moving past the bumps and bruises, it was a different time growing up in Miami Beach back in the 60's and early 70's. At an early age we had the ability to go throughout the city without the worry that someone was going to "get us." We used to walk to school, get on the C bus, and go to Lincoln Road to walk around and see a movie. I'll skip the part of the price of the movie (double feature), the popcorn, and the soda, as my kids might throw up if they see it in print–as they've probably heard it a thousand times. We were young when we were allowed to do those things. I'm talking elementary school age.

I remember walking to elementary school past WQAM, 560 on the AM radio dial, and meeting all the DJs especially, Rick Shaw, a South Florida legend. They were the first to play the Beatles in Miami, had a GTO painted like a tiger (with a tail), and Rick even had a TV show where local teens would lip sync to the Supremes and others. Funny thing was, that on the TV show, the Supremes were three white girls. It was the late 60's. Don't ask me why, but I have a vivid memory of a kid by the name of Bobby, lip syncing to the song "Lightning Strikes" while standing on top of the diving board at the Deauville Hotel.

Those who know me know that I love music and would not be surprised that I have maintained that memory. Joy is probably sick of me asking her when a tune comes on if she knows the song's name and the artist. I usually know it within a few notes. Growing up, I played trumpet and we even tried to start a band like Chicago or Blood, Sweat and Tears. After one practice, we abandoned the idea.

In my teen years, my mother decided to remodel the house, and I was able to talk her into black carpet for my room. I combined that with a four-wall collage imbedded with Playboy pin-ups. That went along with the Lava lamps, black lights, and lights that flashed to the music. The final piece was an old barrel that was painted black, drilled with holes that said, "Make love not war." It had lights inside that lit up the wording in the dark. It was the 70's, and I was fully entrenched in it.

3440 Meridian even held a few secrets. My dad never knew it, but I knew where he hid the key to his closet, and yes, he kept it locked. I'd use the key from time to time for this or that. I'd open it up to steal a few dollars from his money stash to help augment my allowance. I didn't get much from him, which is one of the reasons I started working at the age of 13. Since our points of view on just about everything were on opposite sides of the spectrum, I needed that money and a job for a little bit of independence from my dad.

The other thing I used to break in for was to get the key to my aunt's apartment at the Triton Towers. She only used the apartment part of the year, so I availed myself of it the rest of the time. I finally got smart, and rather than get caught stealing the keys, I took them down to the corner hardware store and had my own set made. I sometimes used that apartment as a rendezvous point with my first girlfriend, Susie.

Me and Susie, freshmen year of high school

We were a couple in middle school (7th to 9th grades). At that age we were not old enough to drive, so on a Saturday we'd both take different city buses and meet at a friend's house, Lincoln Road, the beach or at the apartment. The funny part about the apartment was that since my aunt only lived there part of the year, and in Philadelphia the rest of the year, when she left she loaded the place up with mothballs. This helped deal with the humidity because she turned the air conditioner up high. The place stunk really bad for the first few minutes, until we opened the windows and aired it out. Susie and I didn't care since we could hangout together, and no one ever bothered us there.

So yes, that house on Meridian Avenue had a lot of memories, the good, the bad and the ugly. Betty was right-on about that night we moved in—staying there the first night brought us good luck. When my parents moved with my brother to Las Vegas in 2000, they sold the house, or I should say my father sold the house over the objections of my mother for $300,000. Not a bad profit from a $19,500 purchase price in 1962.

When I'm in Miami Beach, I usually do a "drive by" of the old house just to see what's been done to the place. The people my parents sold it to kept it for about five years, and they sold it for about $650,000. I've always thought that at some point in time, I might get the courage to knock on the door and ask to come in and see the place, one last time.

On a recent Sunday my brother sent me a text with a picture of the house at 3440, and the text said, "Open house today." It seemed that the old homestead was on the market again. We quickly made plans to go to the open house, to see it one last time.

My daughter Melissa, my son Jeff, Joy and I, met my brother Warren at the house that afternoon. The new owners had fixed up the downstairs really nice, modernizing the kitchen, bathroom, and floors. They also made a new master bath, on what was an open sun porch. All the new things aside, it was great to stand in my old room and reminisce, and at last bring some final closure.

The house is now on the market for $1.2 million...I guess we should have kept it.

My Bar Mitzvah—Mom, Me, and Dad

Dining Out—Mid 1970's. Me, Mom, Warren and Dad.

Relatives Visit

Since my parents were the only ones to leave Philadelphia, during the winter months we had a slew of visitors escaping the great white north. Some were fun to have around, and some were a pain in the you-know-what, as they outstayed their welcome (at least according to me).

My father's sister Mollye and her husband Morris liked Miami Beach so much, that they got a place at the Triton Towers and stayed all season from October to April, escaping the cold. Having Aunt Mollye and Uncle Morris down for half the year was great for my mother, as she and Mollye made a formidable pair against Lenny. Since Mollye was his older sister, my mom would tell her what she wanted, and look out, it always worked out just the way they'd planned. He'd get so pissed knowing that he'd been had.

Morris and Mollye, my closest aunt and uncle growing up

We'd go out to dinner with them almost every night. Whenever we'd go to pick them up, Mollye would be there, but not Morris. He'd be out walking while he was waiting for us. He was always walking, to the point of it being a little crazy.

We had such great times with them, and I became very close to them and to their daughter Barbara, husband Dave, and their kids, Stephi, Stuart and Sally. They would come down over the winter holidays and just lie in the sun. Today I always say Barbara is like my second mom, since her kids are all around my

Cousin Barbara and her daughter Stephi - 1983

age, and I lived with her a couple months a year while going to college in Philadelphia. We are still very close today. In 2013, we lost Stephi to a heart attack at age 56. For all who knew her and for her immediate family, it was a tough blow as she was always a part of our lives.

Stephi was special. She was severely handicapped and did not walk or talk, but you could communicate with her, and she ALWAYS gave me smiles and hugs when she saw me. She was not treated as special, just one of the family, and was included in everything we did. She enriched us all, and I truly miss her.

Back to the visits...

One story stands out about Mollye and Morris. You see, Morris had a detached retina. Back in the early 1970's that was pretty dangerous for loss of sight, and Mollye was a little

Mollye, Barbara, Me, Melissa, Chuck, Sally, Dave and Ben - 2013

over protective about him getting hit in the head. Actually, she was more than just a little over protective. One time we went to see Tony Bennett at the Diplomat Hotel. It must have been a New Year's Eve show since Barbara was also there. Well, Mollye made sure Morris was out of harm's way so nothing could fall on him because of his detached retina, and she insisted he switch seats with her. Next thing we know, at the end of dinner, the waiter drops an ice cream parfait right on Mollye's head. It dripped down her face and her dress. After about ten seconds of silence, we all broke into laughter as she had insisted on taking THAT seat.

Then there was my father's brother, Joe. I think everybody has an Uncle Joe. He was a retired dentist, who came down for the winter, in his later years. Uncle Joe had two big problems: One, he inherited the family disease of Retinitis Pigmentosa and was nearly blind. I was the lucky one chosen to lead him around whenever we went out, which was every night. We were at Pumpernick's (famous restaurant on Miami Beach) waiting in line, and when we were called, I forgot him and walked to the table. Well, the next thing we hear from way across the restaurant is, "Where is that little son of a bitch?" That would be me, since I left him. Then everyone in the restaurant stopped what they were doing and looked over to Uncle Joe and me, and I was so embarrassed.

Edith, Uncle Joe, Lenny and me
circa 1957

Uncle Joe's other problem, like a lot of people in his generation, was that he was bigoted. That, combined with no eyesight, was a terrible combination. You never knew when he would say the wrong thing to the wrong person. One time Barbara and I went to visit him in a nursing home where he shared a room with a very nice African-American man. Needless to say, with the combination of no eye sight and his bigotry, we were horrified of what he might say to this nice man, not knowing he was African-American.

The last story really ties together the visits and my father's eccentricities. My dad would shuttle relatives to and from the airport, and on this one day he was taking Barbara and her family to the airport, with Uncle Morris and me along for the ride. We were actually in two cars, and as we crossed the first bridge on the Julia Tuttle Causeway, one of the vehicles got a flat tire. Not catastrophic unless, of course, you were in one of our cars.

My father liked to get things that "fell off the truck." That included spare tires. So we go to put on the spare and guess what? It didn't fit. You ask why it didn't fit? Well, you see, it was stolen off a rental car that was thought to be the same as our car. We hailed a cab to take Barbara and her family to the airport. When I returned for Uncle Morris, he was gone. I looked up, and he was walking over one of the tallest bridges in Miami, against traffic, with only a couple of feet to spare between him, the cars, and being blown off into Biscayne Bay.

Recently, I was told an unbelievable story that really made me laugh. The story is about how Uncle Joe got from that nursing home in Atlantic City to Philadelphia, after he had passed away. Then again, knowing my father, it really was not that surprising. Apparently, the funeral home wanted what my father believed was too much money to transport Uncle Joe's body to Philadelphia for burial. So in typical Lenny fashion, he hired a limo and propped up Uncle Joe for the hour-long ride to the funeral home in Philadelphia. It reminded me of the movie *Weekend at Bernie's*!

Miami Beach ~ Fun in the Sun

The Algiers Hotel, Miami Beach

From the time I was an infant until I turned seven, we had a cabana for the summer at the Algiers Hotel. It's there that I learned to swim at the early age of two. I was always intrigued by the guy who taught me to swim, especially when I met him again in my early teens. His nickname was Froggie, and I never did know his real name. He was your typical beach bum. I'm using that term, but he just never left the beach. He was around the ocean and the pools teaching swimming and scuba diving his whole life, without a care in the world. He was quite a character. Besides swimming, he had me jumping off the high board when I was three, and then he used me in exhibitions to get more business.

At age eight, my parents decided to step it up a notch, and we left the Algiers for a cabana at the Fontainebleu Hotel. Although

The Fountainebleu Hotel, Miami Beach

its heyday was the 50's and early 60's, it was still a pretty happening place in the late 60's too. Many movies were filmed there, but the two that come to mind were James Bond's "Goldfinger" and "Catch Me if You Can," about the great imposter and forger,

Frank Abagnale. Not to get too far off the current subject, but I met Frank Abagnale in the early 90's after the FBI caught him, and he'd turned his knowledge of how to commit forgery into a business. He sold his services to companies and taught them how to strengthen their controls and protect against check fraud. Tony Curtis played him in the original movie, and Leonardo DiCaprio played him in the remake of the movie.

My parents and another family, the Dansky's, split the $600 fee for the cabana for the summer. Warren and I used to have the run of the place with all of its amenities. At that time, the hotel had indoor and outdoor swimming pools, an ice skating rink, 10 bowling lanes, and a youth staff that provided daily activities for all the kids.

Our Rabbi even had a cabana several cabanas down from us. My parents would drop us off, then pick us up at the end of the day, if they weren't staying. Usually, they would stay and give us a certain time to be ready to leave for home. Warren would always test those limits. On one particular summer day my father had had enough of waiting for him, so we all packed up and left without him. The rabbi looked at my dad and said, "How can you leave him to walk home? He's only seven or eight."

My father told the Rabbi in no uncertain terms to mind his own business, and that he was going to teach his son a lesson. Well, Warren walked home crying all the way. You might ask, how do I know that, and the answer is simple. My father wanted to teach him a lesson, but not put him in harm's way. We followed him the two miles home, in the car, and he never knew we were watching him. After that day, he was never late.

One of my favorite things to do was, of course, swim, but I was one of the few who also made use of the ten meter diving platform.

I was brave back then and not much stopped me from doing what I wanted to do. That bravery almost came back to bite me one day. I got into an argument with some guy in the pool, and the dude tried to drown me. I finally broke away from him, but when I brought one of the lifeguards back to point him out, he was gone.

Another favorite activity of mine was ice skating. The rink at the hotel was small, but it was fun nonetheless. Since it was a round sheet of ice, we'd race around in circles all day. I was a pretty good skater, but due to that rink, I only learned how to do crossovers one way, which later became a hindrance when I coached my son's ice hockey team.

Me ice skating at The Fountainebleu Hotel circa 1968

Even though I loved to skate, there were two instances that threatened that love. Once I was helping a girl to skate, and I was holding her and pushing her from behind. She fell, and I accidently ran over a couple of her fingers with my skates. She was hurt pretty bad, and I was really scared. I ran and hid in the cabana the rest of the day. Her parents wanted to sue, but nothing ever came of that. It was, after all, just an unfortunate accident.

The other instance happened after I stopped going to the Fontainebleu on a regular basis, because I started to work as a pool boy at another hotel. In this case, I had not been to the Fontainebleu cabana for months, but I'd left my ice skates there. So I showed up at the cabana one day, grabbed my ice skates, and even though I didn't have any socks with me, I decided I was going to skate anyway. I went to the rink, laced up the skates, got out on the ice, and then suddenly I felt something moving in my skate.

Now anyone who lives in Florida knows not to leave anything out for a while, as the bugs are horrendous. Well, I got off the ice as fast as I could, took my skates off as fast as I could, and a much unwanted guest came crawling out—a huge Palmetto bug! That ended my skating early, and I seriously didn't skate again for a long time after.

My parents kept the cabana for several more years, but that year was the last for me, as I was too busy working poolside at the Algiers.

Just a side note: the Fontainebleu pool area was remodeled in the 80s' or 90's, and the ice skating rink is gone, as well as the cabanas. The Olympic size pool and diving platforms were replaced with a free-formed pool with swim-up bars and lots of palm trees. Progress, I guess.

Pool Boys

The Algiers

When I turned 13, my father and I decided it was time for me to find a part-time job to earn some of my own money. He called an old friend of his, Danny Wolf. Danny was the pool manager at the Algiers Hotel, and my father asked him to hire me as a pool boy. I was pretty comfortable with the situation since I had learned to swim at the Algiers, 11 years earlier when I was about two years old.

Danny hired me right away. I'd go after school to pick up mats and towels, sweep up the day's cigarette butts and other assorted garbage, and close up the cabanas. For this I got $5 a day. If I worked on the weekends, I'd get $15 for the whole day, 8 am to 5 pm. It was a good gig.

Danny had a couple of partners, Perry and Phil. Phil was a really nice man, who catered to the hotel guests, just as well as Danny. But Danny also knew the pool operations, which I'd soon learn was a real challenge for a large, salt water pool. Then there was Perry. I don't even know where to start with that one. He was nice enough, but his sole responsibility was to manage the "gambling operation." Yes, I said gambling.

The guys paid off the Miami Beach cops and ran high stakes poker games right on the pool deck. They took a cut of every hand, and ran drinks, food, cigars and cigarettes, and fresh cards to the games, all day long. We did run afoul of the law one time when the payoff wasn't on time, and the cops shut us down for a week or so. No matter, we moved the games to the hotel roof in the interim, with no break in the action.

Now I ask you, do you think my father set me up there for a reason? I think he was trying to make me "street smart." No matter, it didn't take, as I'm as honest as the day is long, and I have preached integrity to my kids since they were old enough to understand the concept. I did, however, learn to run card games, which would prove useful at another pool when I was in college.

I went from pool boy to lifeguard over the years, but I still did the pool boy job because it was Danny's, Phil's and Perry's place. The setup of the Algiers had the pool separated from the beach by a boardwalk that ran between the hotels and the beach for about six blocks. We had a lifeguard on the beach, but when he pushed an alarm that meant he had a swimmer in trouble, and we would all come running.

I remember one time in particular where the undercurrent or riptide was very strong. There was not one, but four swimmers from the same group in trouble. We each grabbed surfboards and went out after them. Once we rescued them, one of them turned to us and said, "My friend is still out there." There were five, not four. Well, we looked and looked, as did the Coast Guard, but it was too late. We lost him. In all likelihood he was gone before we went after the original four. He washed up two hotels down, the next morning. It was not a pretty sight, and we all felt terrible that a family was going home without one of their loved ones. Thankfully, in all the years I worked at various pools, that was the only time we lost someone.

One other time this guy came up to me at the pool. He was wearing sunglasses, and he said, "I lost my glass eye when I dove in. Can you find it for me?" I thought he was kidding, but he wasn't. So I got my mask and snorkel and dove into the pool. It took about ten minutes, but I found it, gave it to him, and he hit me with a $5 tip. What a cheap bastard. The replacement glass

Life on the Beach

eye was probably going to cost him hundreds, maybe more, to replace. Oh well, it was still a good deed.

The Algiers was a cool place to be for the summertime and holidays. It was full of families and kids/teens that would come down from the north for vacation—some for a week. For others, the husbands would stay for a week and then leave the family for the whole summer while they went back to work. Summertime had counselors and activities planned for all ages. Even though I was working there, I would also help out with the activities such as chaperone trips to Michelle's Go Carts or Putt Putt golfing.

The hotel also did pool parties once a week at night. The pool boys would be on guard for the parties. We got paid by being able to go to the dining room kitchen and get anything we wanted for dinner. Those pool parties were the best for meeting girls and hanging out. Being a teen myself, I did the job to meet girls, of which there were plenty over the years.

Two summers stand out for me for different reasons: 1970 and 1972. In 1970, Miami Beach had a program called Young Summer 70, where they sponsored free concerts once a week on the lawn in front of the Convention Center. I got a job with the city for those events, and I worked the stage area helping set up for bands like The Allman Brothers, Tavares, Cornelius Brothers and Sister Rose, and Alive and Kicking. As I loved music, it was really cool.

The other summer, 1972, was a wild one. Both the Democratic and Republican National Conventions were held in Miami Beach, and all the hippies and other assorted protesters showed up. It was a strange happening. My parents went away during the first convention and left me to stay on my own at my aunt's vacant apartment, just a few doors down from the Algiers. That led to party time at the apartment—booze, pot and girls.

My parents were back for the second convention, but they decided it would be a good idea for the family to get out of town. So they took us to this new park that had just opened up. You may have heard of it, Walt Disney World's Magic Kingdom. Part of me wanted to stay back and enjoy the Convention at my aunt's, just like during the first convention. But part of me wanted to go see this new amusement park. It was fun, but, of course, on the way up, my dad had to make a business stop. No surprise there. That would be the first of about 100 or more trips to Walt Disney World.

As they say, "All good things must come to an end," and the Algiers was no exception. It closed down in my senior year of high school. It was torn down to make way for a condominium.

Before it closed, I met Muhammad Ali at the hotel. He was staying there for a number of months as he trained for a title fight at the famous 5th Street Gym, with the famous Angelo Dundee,

Me and a co-worker, Scott

Me working hard...

Danny M (co-worker), Fran (guest) and Me

another man my father knew well.

Crystal House

After the Algiers closed, I went to work with Phil, who got the pool manager's job at the Crystal House. He had finally learned and passed the test to get his pool manager's license. It was a short stay for me as this was a condo pool, and not much excitement to be had.

Harbor Island Spa

The Harbor Island Spa was next for me. The pool manager was a real character named Jack. He was yet another acquaintance of my father's. At the time I was attending Miami Dade Junior College, and I smoked Marlboro cigarettes. He used to show me pictures of dirty lungs, trying to get me to quit. However, put a drink in his hand, and the sucker became a chain smoker of Lucky Strikes, without filters no less. He also had no clue how to run a pool, even though he was the pool manager. That left me to take care of the pool pumps, backwash the filters, and balance the chemicals of a large saltwater pool. Good thing Danny taught me well at the Algiers.

It was here that my previous experience with running card games came into play, once more. Unlike the poker games at the Algiers, we were running some high stakes gin games at the pool. Since this was a "friendly" game between guests, we didn't have to pay off the cops, nor did we get a cut on every pot. However, we did charge a markup for all the food, drinks, cigarettes, cigars and cards we got for the players. With that and a healthy tip on each game, combined with the tips from the regular pool operations, I did rather well. It allowed me to purchase my first car, a brand new 1973 Buick Century Luxus, for $3,995.

When I left town to go to Temple University in Philadelphia, my pool boy days were over.

Stoner Days

I could start and end this chapter by saying, unlike Bill Clinton, I did inhale.

I don't remember how or when I started (those brain cells are gone), but I did. I never did any other drugs, but I did smoke some weed over the years in some unique places.

Me age 16

In high school, I had an algebra class where the teacher had to come from the portable classrooms on the other side of the school, and he was always late. A few of us would smoke a roach, and he'd come in and say, "Gee, the electrical system in this building has to get fixed. It sure smells." Don't know if he was really that dumb, or if he just didn't care.

A friend's father owned an apartment house next to the Netherlands Hotel, which they also lived in. Although we had some places to smoke over at the Netherlands (the roof, the kitchen and the basement), it was nothing like the setup we had over at the apartment house. The first place we had was sort of "in the basement." You see, we went through the basement, and then through a little duct door into some crawl space under the building, which we had dug out. By removing the sand, we had a space with enough headroom to sit in chairs and hide away. We had a TV and a fan in there to keep it from being "hot as hell."

While that was nice for a bit, we had bigger plans. Up on the roof there was a four-foot wall all around the building. My friend got the bright idea that he could build a room up on the roof, and no one would know. So he did. It was approximately ten feet by ten feet built of wood, and it had a metal roof, not unlike the kind of buildings you see in impoverished neighborhoods in third world countries. It also had an air conditioner—a definite step up from a fan—plus a TV and a stereo, a couch, a recliner, and a lamp. It had all the comforts of home. There was even an elaborate alarm system with a rope and a bell, so we would know when anyone was coming past the third floor, up to the roof.

That room made it through all of high school and into our college years. Many a Saturday Night Live, with the original cast, was watched from that room, and many a joint or bong was smoked. If you have seen "That 70's Show," our place looked like the basement scene right out of that show, although we were actually experiencing it in the 70's.

Fortunately for us, when the munchies hit, we had Butterflake Bakery on the next block. We would walk over and buy a pound or so of butter cookies with sprinkles. When we were really munch'n, we would buy a whole cheesecake and a half-gallon of milk and head back to "the room" for some serious eating. Never mind that we didn't have a knife to cut the cheesecake or plates to eat it on. We'd just take a book of matches and cut it by however many people were there, and munched it down until there was nothing left.

Then there was my best friend's house. He had moved into the converted garage, and the pot flowed daily there. His mom was oblivious. There, we really did have all the comforts of home, because it was home.

Besides the permanent smoking locations, we did travel some. One time it almost got me busted. I was driving down Alton Road at night, and there were four of us in the car with two joints going when I got pulled over by the police. Recognizing that I had a serious problem on my hands, I got out and went over to the cop's car, something that you can't do today. I said, "Officer, what's the problem?" hoping all the while he didn't smell anything on me.

He said, "Do you know why I stopped you?"

I said, "No, I thought I was driving within the speed limit."

He then said, "You are driving without your headlights."

I was thinking, Man I'm stoned, I don't need no stinking headlights.

He then said, "Please put them on and be careful driving."

I said, "Thank you," and was on my way. I dodged a real bullet that day.

I started cruising the Caribbean in the middle 70's. Cruising back then was way different than it is today. One could say that was the "wild west" of cruising. Back then we used to be allowed to party with the crew, unlike today where the crew is kept separate from the guests. I remember one trip where we partied with the Jamaican bar staff, smoked ganja, and drank beer all night long. I learned some Jamaican words that night that I still remember to this day, though they are not repeatable. "Ire, yeah mon!!!"

During the same high school time period, we also got into gambling. We turned into a bunch of degenerates, spending all our money at the various dog tracks, Miami Jai Alai, and betting on football games. We were always looking for that big score. A few hundred dollars a night, back then, was big. We'd go during the week on school nights, and on the weekends as well. After a night at Biscayne Kennel Club, I was dropping off my friend Alan at his apartment on South Beach, when two cops pulled us over and held us at gunpoint. It seemed that we looked like two suspects that had just committed a murder, no less. So they pulled us over to check us out. They let us go, but not before searching the car (no probable cause rules back then), and of course, they came up with a roach and a roach clip, and they threatened to take us in. They were just trying to bully us. But being held at gunpoint is an interesting feeling, one which I never care to experience again.

While at the tracks, we sought advice on betting from a bunch of old-time degenerates that seemed to know what they were doing. Looking back on it, I guess they really didn't know any more than we did, as they never hit it big either. It was sad really, as they were grown men, and that was what their lives had turned into. Honestly, I can now say I don't gamble. I have only stepped into a casino a few times to look around, and I've have never been back to a dog track or to Jai Alai since I was married. My money is my money, and I'll be dammed if I'm just going to give it up for nothing in return.

Through it all, I came through those crazy years pretty much unscathed. However, looking back at it from a drug standpoint, I was one of the lucky ones because I never did anything other than smoke a little pot. In the end though, we all survived "the 70's."

Stu, Me, and Ted in our post high school stoner days

A Philadelphia Connection

College Begins at Home

Thanks to a program called the Quinmester, I went to high school a couple of summers and was able to finish high school in November of my senior year. Having just turned 17 and not really having the grades, I turned to Miami Dade Community College (MDCC) to further my education. However, that's not really the full story.

You see, back in the day, at least in my family, there was no studying for the SATs or ACTs. In fact, nobody knew about them. We were told at school that we were taking a long-ass test, and to show up. So we did, and boy, did I suck at that test. I think my combined score didn't equal one part of the scores my kids have received. They studied and took prep classes...times are different.

I actually owe my mom for all that I am today, as she was the one to fight my dad to allow me the opportunity to go to college. He thought I was too dumb, and he told me so on a number of occasions.

So off to MDCC I went, majoring in biology. I wanted to be a doctor. Not any type of doctor, but an optometrist. Yeah, just like my dad–imagine that. My daughter thinks this was because I was still trying to please him. Although once again, since he didn't like being an optometrist, he discouraged me. He kept saying that they didn't make any money, and that I needed to find something else. Certainly, if I had continued to pursue it, my life would be totally different. For starters, I would have never met my wife. Ah the twists and turns that fate plays in all our lives, with every decision we make.

I did well at MDCC, turning my high school grade point average of 2.3 into a college GPA of 3.8. As fate would have it, while at MDCC and working at the Harbor Island Spa as a pool boy, I had to go to some lame play my brother was in at the Temple we belonged to. It was "Fiddler On The Roof," and my brother played Perchik. If you know the story, one of Tevia's daughters, Hodel and Perchik fall in love. When I saw the girl playing opposite him as Hodel, I was immediately struck by her and just had to find out her name, age (important back then), and of course, did she have a boyfriend.

Me and Suzy in my college years circa 1976

It turned out that her name was Suzy, she was 15 (I was 17), and she didn't have a boyfriend. You see she had just moved to Miami Beach from Philadelphia. In the Dade County School system, 9th grade was in junior high, and high school began at 10th grade. But truly, if you looked at it the way I did, even though I was in college (during my senior year of high school) and she was in 9th grade, I was really a senior in high school, and she was a freshman. So not so bad, right?

So Suzy and I dated for about a year. Unknown to me when we started dating, her father was only here on a one to two year assignment from his company. They ended up moving back to Philadelphia.

I ended up with huge phone bills, and I traveled back and forth to Philadelphia to see her. I guess her parents liked me as they let me stay at their house when I visited. They even introduced me to Philly cheesesteaks and took me to Atlantic City just to get a cheesesteak at the famous place called the White House, which I still visit today.

I also spent a summer up in Philadelphia. It was a bit much to ask her parents to put me up for such a long period. A friend of theirs agreed to rent me a room close by, for cheap. It was a nice house, and the people were nice, but they had this big old St. Bernard. You do know what those dogs are famous for, and it's not carrying a whiskey barrel around their neck and rescuing people in the snow. NO–IT'S THEIR SLOBBER!!!

I swear there was dog slobber everywhere: on the floors, on the walls, everywhere. However, the funniest story about that summer was something that dog did one day when I was the only one home. He was huge, well over a hundred pounds, and this one afternoon he got out of the house. I can't to this day figure out how, but that was just the beginning of his amazing feat. Next door there was a Doberman in a very tall, fenced pen in the back yard. I guess she was in heat since the next thing I saw was this huge St. Bernard squeezing under the gate into the pen. The pen maybe had three inches of clearance between it and the ground. Don't know how he got his body to do it, but he got in, and well, I'll let you imagine the rest. Too bad we didn't have iPhones back then as the video would have gone viral.

After that summer I returned to Miami for one last semester at MDCC.

Back to Philadelphia

People always ask me how did I end up going to Temple University? It was really several factors. First, Suzy and I were still dating. Second, I wanted to get away from home, and lastly it was cheap for my father. You see being born in Philadelphia and using my cousin Barbara's address, the University made a mistake and gave me state residency rates. Lucky for Dad.

Also lucky for Dad was the fact that his sister had an apartment in Philadelphia and an apartment in Miami Beach, which she used from mid-October to mid-April. That left the Philadelphia apartment vacant for most of the school year. He got her to agree to let me stay there when she was in Miami Beach. On the fringe months, during the start and end of the school year, I lived with my cousin Barbara and her family. Thus, Barbara, and the rest of her family, became my closest relatives, and she has always given me the feeling, then and now, that she was like my second mom.

Barbara treated me like a son and made me feel right at home. A story she tells to this day, was the time I had just come back from Wawa where I had picked up Tastycakes and soda for myself, (I can still see it as if it happened yesterday). She leaned out an upstairs window and told me to go to Wawa to get her some milk. My response was typical for a lazy college kid, and I said, "I just came from there, and I don't want to go back." Her response was also typical for Barbara, and she said, "I don't give a damn where you just were, go to Wawa and get me some milk." So of course, off I went, back to Wawa.

Suzy and I were still dating when I was at Temple. I used to pick her up after class at Cheltenham High School and go to her football games, as she was a cheerleader. Some of the kids gave her a hard time since she was dating a college guy. She just ignored them.

That first semester at Temple, I was still Pre-Med and one of my classes was Genetics. The professor starts the first day with, "Only 25 percent of you will pass this class." He was right. Along with the class came a genetics lab worth two credit hours. I was spending 10 to 12 hours a week in this stupid lab when I realized that this was not for me. I was part of the 75 percent that dropped the class.

When my aunt came back from Florida, I moved back to Barbara's, but I also had to figure out what I was going to do next, since I was going to change my major. Suzy's father helped me get a job for the summer working at Baker Shoes selling women's shoes, of all things.

I got a real world experience of working for a living and having to pay my own bills. I rented an apartment not far from Oxford Valley Mall. Barbara's house was not an option, as it was too far away.

While working there, the manager actually taught me how to make a tie, another life lesson. The women would want to try on everything, and then only buy one pair, or maybe nothing. The salesmen had a rule: three pairs, and then we didn't have their size in whatever they asked for. We didn't want to get tied up with one non-buyer, we needed volume to make our numbers.

There were ladies that brought their sick kid(s) with them. While you were helping the lady put on the shoe, you were at just the right height for the kid to sneeze in your face. That was lovely. Then there were the ladies that wanted boots. OH BOOTS!! Of course the shoe would fit, but pulling up the zipper over their always fat calf, now that there is an experience. One lady actually brought pliers with her for leverage on the zipper!! Unbelievable.

That experience had me RUNNING right back to school. I took some summer courses in accounting and thought that I liked it. I could make short order of it, much better than genetics and eight more years of college. So off I went into the Temple Business

School to take Accounting.

At that early stage, I had no idea what that would mean for me. I knew nothing about the CPA designation, and nothing about what kind of job I could land with it. All I knew was that it was shorter time than Pre-Med and medical school, to get out and start working.

It was about that time that Suzy and I started having some issues. Looking back on it, I was too controlling and immature. What a revelation...I was 20. We broke up that year, although we stayed in touch and saw each other from time to time while I was still in Philadelphia.

Even though I was in school, I still continued to work at Baker Shoes and then at A.S. Beck to make a little extra money. I got so good at it that I was also a specialist for opening new stores. I opened stores at Montgomery Mall, Lehigh Valley Mall in Allentown, and several stores out of state, as far away as Virginia.

Instead of working through the holidays my junior year, I went home for about a month for winter break and worked at a pool to make a little money, and of course, meet girls. When I got back to my apartment in Philadelphia, a day before the winter semester was to start, I found my car plowed in. So here is my "I walked to school in the snow story," that every parent tells their kids.

It wasn't quite like that, but since the car had not been started in a month, the heater did not work on the 45-minute drive to the Temple Ambler campus. When I got there, the parking lot had not been plowed, and we had to park on the street. I had about a mile hike into the campus. When I got in there, I found out classes were cancelled. I spent the next couple of hours in the student union, by the fire, warming up before braving the walk and ride back to my apartment. By the way, the heat in my car started working on the way back.

The "U"

The summer between my junior and senior year, I had to take a lot of courses to catch up in the Business School, if I wanted to graduate on time, since I had changed my major from Pre-Med. That led me to come home to Miami Beach and enroll in the University of Miami for the summer. I ended up being on campus from 7:30 in the morning until 10:00 at night, taking four accounting classes, two in each six-week summer session. I took one class in the morning, and one at night, and spent the day in the library studying and sleeping. Doing it that way, allowed me to have my weekends free...and what a summer that was.

I met a girl in the early part of the summer at a random hotel on Miami Beach, I think it was actually the Holiday Inn. There was a bar where the band was playing Jimmy Buffet songs, so we hung out there. She was from PA, close to school, so we hit it off for a few days, and then she went home. About two months later at my friend's hotel in South Beach, I met and dated another girl from PA. After about a couple of days, the girl asks me if I had met anyone else from PA that summer. I thought that was a random question, but I said "Yes." Then she says the girl's name, and again I said, "Yes." Then she says, "That's my sister." Crazy coincidence!!

A couple of nights later we were in the Forge Restaurant and Bar on Miami Beach at about 2 a.m. with a bunch of others partying when gunshots rang out. We all ducked under the tables as someone wrestled with the gunman to get his gun. They got him, and held him for the cops. The next thing I know is that my date, who was a nurse, jumped up and started working on the guy who had been shot, trying to keep him alive until the paramedics got there.

He died the next day. His name was Craig Teriaca, who I believe was in the family of Angelo Bruno, the Philadelphia Mob boss.

Just a side note, a lot of Philadelphia connections kept making appearances in my life.

The guy who shot him was Richard Schwartz, Meyer Lansky's stepson, yet another crazy connection–not to Philadelphia, but to my adopted father. Meyer was the Jewish Mob boss in South Florida, who my father knew, based on the book making business he was involved in. They arrested Schwartz, and then let him out on bail. He was killed a short time later when he was machine gunned down in front of another popular restaurant in Bay Harbor Islands.

Out From the Cold

In my senior year, my aunt became sick, and we knew over the summer that she would not be back to Florida, so I had to find a place to live. I ended up sharing a two-bedroom apartment in Hatfield, PA with three other guys, only one of whom was in school.

Hatfield was a special place. It was primarily known for its slaughterhouse called Hatfield Meats. On a bad day, you could smell the place all the way into the apartment. No wonder it was so cheap!

The year was uneventful except for two things. First, the winter of 1978 was known for its cold, snow and ice storms. Those storms drove my decision to go back to Florida. Second, I was offered a position in public accounting by the firm of Grant Thornton, with a choice of Miami or Philadelphia. That was a no brainer–Miami, of course.

The funny thing about getting a job in public accounting, it was just a matter of a chance casual conversation with a classmate. I had no idea about the "Big 8" firms interviewing on campus. In fact, I didn't even know what the "Big 8" was until he told me. I thought that would be a good place to start my career, so I signed up for the on-campus interviews, and I got two offers. Amazing how "chance conversations" or a little bit of information can change your whole life.

I graduated from Temple in May 1978, drove home, and went on a short cruise with some college friends before I had to start work later that month. After the cruise, I came home to an empty house, only to find a note my dad had left for me: "Mom and I are in Philadelphia–Aunt Mollye passed away (my father's sister), and Aunt Ethel (my mother's sister) passed away, as well, a few hours apart." I was closest with my Aunt Mollye, as I've mentioned previously, I'd used both her apartment in Miami Beach and the one in Philadelphia at various points in my life.

The balance of the summer was an absolute blur. I started work and quickly realized that after being on my own in college, along with my father's tough personality, I could no longer live another minute under my father's roof. Much to his disgust, I moved out to a friend's apartment house and rented a small efficiency. He was so pissed that I was paying a friend rent.

At the same time I started a relationship with Betsy, who I knew casually in high school. My mother and her mother were friends, due to their mutual friendship with Betty Chesky.

That short relationship ended in an even shorter engagement. I can honestly say three things about that time. First, Betsy was/is a very nice person, who I can only talk about in a positive light. Second, in some instances I was not a nice guy. I acted towards her like my father sometimes acted towards my mother, even though I knew better. I had to mature some more and unlearn things I had observed about relationships before I could move on with any serious relationship. And third, looking back, it all worked out, as she was clearly not the one for me.

Life, No Longer Just Self

Life Partner

When one thinks about prior decisions made throughout the years, such as going to Philadelphia for a girl and school, changing my major to Accounting from Pre-Med, interviewing for a job on campus, going back to Miami and not getting married, all these decisions and fate led me to my partner, the love of my life, my soul mate. If not for yet another fateful act, we might never have gotten married.

Joy and I met at Grant Thornton when I was in management consulting, traveling around the country on various engagements. She was the Administrative Assistant in the Tax Department having just come over from the IRS. As the story goes, I was working in Atlanta and had been traveling to meet "friends" (girls) in other cities on the weekends, instead of going back to Miami. One particular weekend, I decided to go home, and even though Joy and I had never dated, I asked her to pick me up at the airport, and I would take her to dinner—a first date if you will. She said, "Yes."

During the week, a "friend" from New York invited me to go there instead of going home that weekend. I decided to go for a sure thing, and I broke my date with Joy. I told her that the partner on the job said we were behind and that we had to work the weekend, so I wouldn't be coming back that weekend. I told her we'd get together another time.

Two days later, the girl in New York called my office in Miami and asked the switchboard operator to relay a message to me (no cell phones back then). Since she was new, she turned to Joy for help. The message said, "Something has come up for this weekend, so we'll have to do it another time." Joy told the switchboard operator to give me the message. Then, she waited to see if I'd call to set the date back up with her.

Being the dumbass that I was back then, I thought nothing of it, and called about 30 minutes later.

I said, "The partner called and reconsidered, and we don't have to work the weekend."

Joy said, "Is it that, or did the girl in New York cancel on you?"

I said, "That too."

What a schmuck I was, but I guess in the end it didn't matter as we went out (for the record it was Bagelnosh and about $20). I'd like to say, happily ever after, but that would have to wait.

Wally, Nadia, Joy, and Me in Puerto Rico on the Carnival Festival in 1980

We dated for a few months, took a cruise together, her first one and almost her last. I loved music and dancing, and she wouldn't dance with me the whole cruise. The relationship almost ended right there. We got past the "no dancing," and ended up having a great time. We met lifelong friends on that cruise, Wally and Nadia, again by pure chance. They were seated with us in the dining room, and we struck up enough of a relationship to go on a shore excursion together to a show in Puerto Rico. During the wait for the show, we started to talk about where we went to school, and low and behold, Wally knew and went to school with Joy's brother, Richard. We've been friends ever since.

When we got back from the cruise, Joy moved into my townhouse. I really don't remember how long it was, but after a while I got cold feet and told her I wasn't ready for a long-term relationship. I asked her to move out. She not only moved out, but she quit her job at Grant and went to work for a law firm in downtown Miami. About three weeks later, I came to my senses and sent her flowers with a note. The note said, "I've made up my mind, and I am both sorry and ready." (See, Dear, I do remember the story). She came back to me...and to her job at Grant.

We announced our engagement to our family and kept it a secret at work because otherwise one of us would have had to leave the company. To no one's surprise, her parents were thrilled, and mine were not. My father even went so far as to ask me if she was pregnant–par for the course, for him.

They gave us such a hard time that we ended up eloping and getting married at our townhouse by a notary, who also worked at Grant. We only had her sister present and a couple of friends as witnesses. It was a Thursday night. We both went to work the next day and then to Disney for a couple of days, with a stop in Tampa for me to meet her close friends, now our close friends, Gene and Laura.

Me, Joy, Laura, and Gene at Universal Studios Islands of Adventure in the late 1990's

Our wedding picture. October 23, 1980

When we returned, we told my parents. I'm sure my mom was crushed with no wedding party, but not to worry, it was taken care of twice over. First, Joy's parents threw a party for us at her sister's house, and then a couple of months later, we actually got married again in a small synagogue ceremony with lunch afterwards for about 30 relatives.

Now I can say as of this writing, it's been 35 years and counting.

Our first wedding party in November 1980. Front Row: Joy and Me. Back Row: Our parents: Lenny, Beverly, Bill, and Edith

So what drew me to Joy? If you look back at the start of our relationship some would say that's the wrong question. It was more of what drew her to me. When she came to work for Grant, we first met in the lunchroom and had a lunchtime conversation with a number of other employees present. Although she has never confirmed or denied it, I think it was after that first meeting that she set her sights on me, and then she began to reel me in.

For years she insisted that I only married her because of her car, a 1980 Blue TransAm, just like the one in the Burt Reynold's "Smoky and the Bandit" movie. I have to admit that I did like driving that car. One morning we were going to work in it, and I went through a gas station to avoid a traffic light. A cop pulled us over and gave me a ticket. I later beat the ticket with some quick thinking. After I dropped Joy off at work, I took the car to see a client in Ft Lauderdale.

When I returned to the office, I stopped for gas right down the street from where the cop gave me the ticket. I then went to court and told the judge that when the cop stopped me, I was actually looking for gas, but the price was too high. I produced the receipt for gas, and the judge let me off with a warning. He said, "Next time slow down long enough to make sure the officer knows your intentions." Now that was something my father did like; I guess it was a move he would have made.

All that said, it wasn't the car that drew me to Joy.

So what did attract me to Joy? Yes, she was definitely smart (Type A personality), definitely attractive, and Jewish. Beyond that she was easy to be with. I didn't have to make any effort to pretend to be somebody that I wasn't—we just fit like a fine glove on a hand. I had never felt that way before. We were friends and lovers, and we still are. She is my best friend, my biggest supporter, no matter what. Sure we rub each other the wrong way from time to time. The kids still talk about the time we threw hamburgers and salad at each other, but I couldn't picture my life without her. Actually, there is no doubt about it—I love her even more today than when we were married.

Being into music, several songs come to mind here. She will probably hate these references since I quiz her all the time when songs come on the radio: Spiral Staircase's "I love you more today than yesterday;" Orleans's "You're Still The One;" and Paramore's "Still Into You." They are all truly how I feel.

Even though we swore off spending money on Hallmark cards years ago, as it was a waste of money, she got me a card this year for Valentine's day. Although it cost $3.99 (yes, I turned the card over and looked at the price—I always do) it does sum up our relationship. It said,

"I love how we live, I love what we share, I love who we are together, I love you."

The bottom line is—I would be lost without her!!

Married With Children

It's difficult, to say the least, to try and write about 33 years of parenting, and I'm not about to do it here. It would be too long and too boring. What I would say is this, I think all of us go into it not ready to be a parent, even though we may think we are, and also, we don't want to screw it up. In the end, what I'd hope for was to impart to my children a moral compass–knowing right from wrong, and to stress the importance of education, the importance of self-awareness, and the importance of becoming self-sufficient. At this point I'd have to say, that I'm extremely proud of my children and what they have become. All three are good people, who act with integrity, are compassionate, and I think are happy in their own skin.

So what I will attempt is to convey is the essence of who they are and how they got to what they are in life, through funny stories and even some stories that if fate had gone a different direction, there may not have even been a book to write.

From the beginning, it's been a real ride. Raising three kids was not easy. They all have different personalities, different needs, and different challenges. A post was circulating on Facebook that pretty much sums them up.

About 20 months after we were married, Melissa was born, and life changed forever. Life was no longer about me, but about her. She was born 17 days early, most likely due to the fact that the day before, Joy had chased down our runaway dog, Sonya, tackled her, and carried her back to the house. Sonya was our first dog and was so sweet—a mix between Labrador and Irish Setter.

Since Melissa was born early, her stomach was not fully developed, and she constantly spit up everything she ate. We had to feed her sitting up, and then we put her upright in a baby seat for an hour to make sure she digested her food. One time she began to turn blue because she spit up, and the formula came up both her nose and mouth. I was really freaked out to stay alone with her. But that passed soon enough, and she became a pretty easy child, who we were able to take everywhere.

Sarah, born three years later, had her own unique set of challenges. I would say for months she would cry uncontrollably. We changed her formula multiple times, but nothing helped. We would have to put her in her car seat and drive her around to get her to fall asleep. Then we'd carefully (very carefully) take the car seat out of the car, without removing her, and place it in her crib. NO ONE WANTED TO POKE THE SLEEPING BEAR. Thus her nickname was born—Sarah Beara or SB for short.

Before Jeff was born, we were told we were having another girl. Boy, were they wrong!! We were so excited to have a boy to go along with our two girls. He was perfect. (I can see the girls rolling their eyes as they read this). He had some minor stomach problems and had caught

Sarah, Jeff and Melissa in 1991

a staff infection while in the hospital. I have a video of the girls coming to the hospital to meet their new brother and hold him for the first time. Melissa was no problem, the older sister wanting to take charge. Sarah, well, let's just say Sarah made a face, and you could read her mischievous eyes that said, "How can I get rid of this thing!" The dynamics are still somewhat the same today, but a little different as they've each grown, and their personalities have matured.

In the early years, Joy continued to work, and we shared the drop off and pick up duty from the babysitter's house and school. I remember driving to work in the morning with Melissa in the back seat and Sarah in the front (before airbags), feeding Sarah a bottle with one hand, and driving with the other. Joy would pick them up. When Jeff was born, we had already moved from Miami to Wellington, and Joy had stopped working to take care of the kids.

We had the usual birthday parties, and one unusual one. When Melissa was three, Joy wanted to get a clown for the party. I wasn't as keen on that idea, not wanting to spend too much money. I gave her a budget to stick to, and she did. Well, what it produced was the scariest clown you've ever seen, complete with a holey t-shirt and adult comedy and tricks. He even lit a cigarette in the house for one of those tricks. I recorded the whole scene, and not only did he scare the kids, the looks on the parents' faces was disbelief. We have watched that video over the years and each time it's like—"What were we thinking?"

Vacationing by Land

As the kids grew up, we did many trips in the USA before we started to travel outside the country. Living in Florida, we went to Disney many, many, many times over the years. We had great times at character breakfasts and seeing all the parks. During those trips, I was peed on–once, pooped on–twice, and given the "Sarah Beara stare-down look" more times than I can count. Even the Clydesdale horses got "the look" as they came barreling towards her on Main Street, and she refused to yield. One not so proud parenting moment at Disney was when I forced Sarah to go on the Summit Plummet slide at Blizzard Beach. It scared the hell out of her, and she'll never go on that type of ride again.

We usually all stayed in one room to save a little cash, but that all changed with one eventful night. Melissa was on an air mattress on the floor, and Jeffrey on a rollaway. In the middle of the night I had to go to the bathroom. I tripped and fell on Melissa, who could have really been badly hurt, but luckily she was not. Since then it was two rooms, and now with the spouses and grandkids–it's four.

We spent time at the beach at The Pink Shell in Fort Myers when the kids were little. More recently we've stayed in a rented house at Punta Vedra Beach, which is near St. Augustine. We traveled to the mountains in the Carolinas and the Tennessee Valleys. We rented houses with creeks and deer running through the properties that were spectacular. Melissa claims that on one

Life, No Longer Just Self

of those trips Sarah tried to push her off Grandfather Mountain. A claim I can't corroborate, but it does seem likely, given Sarah's personality—sorry SB, just telling it like it is.

A couple of times we went on long road trips. Looking back at it, I question my logic for such trips. We once drove to Des Moines, Iowa for a Bar Mitzvah. If anyone would have told me the real directions were to drive to Chicago, make a left, then drive seven more hours, I would not have gone. We kept the kids entertained (before there were DVDs in the cars) with a self-made stand that contained a small TV with a VCR that plugged into the cigarette lighter. It also contained an earphone jack with a three-way splitter, so they could listen, and we didn't have to. A God-send.

That contraption actually saved Melissa's life in Kentucky, as it didn't allow Joy to get to her from the front seat. Instead of Melissa getting a beating (just a figure of speech), a bag of chips, pretzels and other assorted snacks got pulverized. Miraculously, we all survived the trip. The next time we went to Iowa, we flew.

We made a couple of other road trips to Pennsylvania, New York and Atlantic City, all fairly uneventful.

Vacationing by Sea

Since Joy and I loved to cruise, we took the kids with us starting at an early age. I think Melissa was seven and Sarah just four when they went on their first cruise. We went on Premiere Cruise Line's, "The Big Red Boat." It was the precursor to today's Disney Cruises, since it had an affiliation with Disney and Disney characters onboard. We actually left Jeff, at six months old, with friends for that long weekend cruise.

We also made one of the dumbest parenting moves ever, letting Melissa go on an island tour with someone she met on the ship. As we were preparing to leave the island, she and the family she was with were nowhere to be found. Talk about a scary moment—your child missing on an island, in a foreign country, with people you don't know. Just as the last tender was to pull away, they came running—just making it. Again, I reiterate, "What were we thinking..."

The first time we took Jeff was on a week's cruise. The first morning out at sea I heard the engines stop, and having been on many cruises, I knew something was up. I could see them lower a lifeboat, so I grabbed my camera and went up on deck. To my amazement, we picked up about 15 Cuban rafters in the middle of the Florida Straits. They were on nothing more than inner tubes tied together with rope, and plywood on top. Talk about being desperate. They were all detained for the length of the cruise, and then I presume returned to Cuba by our government.

The kids have been on numerous cruises throughout the years: to the Caribbean, Central America, Canada, Alaska and Europe.

Mediterranean Cruise, 2005

Rome, Italy, 2005

Marseille, France, 2005

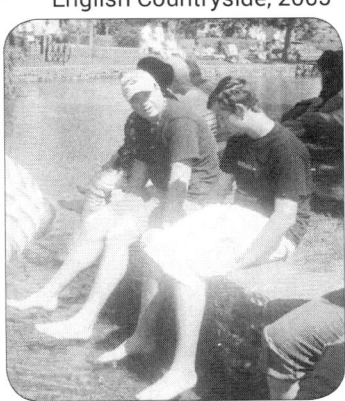
English Countryside, 2005

Blarney Castle, Ireland, 2005

Copenhagen, Denmark, 2006

Flam, Norway, 2008

I only remember my parents taking me to Philadelphia to visit relatives and one trip to Disney. My kids had it rough growing up, didn't they?

Activities

The kids all had activities along the way that they did on their own, or we did together. For the girls, when we lived in Wellington, they did Brownies with their mom. When we moved to Coral Springs, we switched it up, and they did Indian Princesses with me. It was a father and daughter activity group that met once a week for arts and crafts. I hated anytime there was glitter involved, as SB was my child of excess, and it would be all over her and me. The group also went on two sleepaway events, each year. These were held at rustic campsites or ranches with horses, and they played tribal games against each other.

Melissa did cheerleading and basketball in elementary and middle school, and track in high school. Melissa had a love for working on the high school yearbook. She became editor-in-chief her senior year. She went to University of Florida where she met her husband, John. She then finished her education at Florida Atlantic University (FAU) and became a teacher. She taught yearbook (of course) for nine years and now teaches newspaper and English. She has been teaching at the same high school for 12 years.

Sarah was involved with music: playing the piano and then later playing flute in middle school and high school. She went to University of South Florida. After a year of bad grades, a totaled car, and not going to classes, I pulled the plug and gave her the "opportunity" to come home.

It was a rough few months. What we insisted on was either going back to college or finding something that she could do that would make her self-sufficient. She came up with real estate agent (nope), massage therapist (nope), and then paralegal (yep).

We signed her up for the University of Miami Certificate in Paralegal studies program. She loved it so much that she got her Associates Degree in Paralegal Studies, and she is now a certified legal assistant. She's very good at it, and has worked for the same attorney for ten years.

When Jeff was three, he put on roller skates for the first time, and he was a natural skater. That progressed to roller blades and then to ice skates. At five and a half, he began playing ice hockey alongside a number of the Florida Panther players' sons. He played ice hockey until it became a checking league at age 12, and then he played roller hockey throughout his high school and college years. Since I skated, I was always an assistant coach on his teams, up to and including high school. In his senior year of high school, his team won the county championship.

Jeff was nuts in high school. He got this idea to become the Salutatorian for his class of 750, knowing he could not possibly catch his friend, Ralph, for Valedictorian. He took 11 classes a semester, some at high school, some at Florida Atlantic University, and some at Broward College.

He almost got expelled his senior year, not just for taking more classes than he was allowed to take, but because he forged his guidance counselor's signature to get into the extra class. Good thing she really liked Jeff, as she swept it under the rug and just made him drop the extra class. He was mad about it because he had an 'A' in the class. There was no reasoning with him then. However, as he looks back, he now admits it was crazy.

He graduated from high school with a 5.2 GPA and took 54

college credit hours with him to Emory University. It took one and a half years for him to admit he was unhappy there, and needed to leave.

He left for Emory for the winter term, after I begged him not to go back, knowing how unhappy he was. I was delighted when two days later, he phoned me from Tallahassee and said he had enrolled in Tallahassee Community College. That took guts to do.

After one semester, taking a number of different classes to figure out what he really wanted to do, he ended up at Florida State University earning a degree in accounting. He is now a CPA, having worked at Price Waterhouse Coopers, and he is now at Ernst & Young.

I did enjoy myself sharing time with the girls in Indian Princess and sharing time with Jeff in hockey.

A Higher Power

As kids grow up, events happen that shape their lives. We were very fortunate on a number of occasions that either a higher power or perhaps my mother-in-law was watching over them from heaven.

The first of these incidents happened right after my mother-in-law passed away from cancer. My father-in-law had enough of sitting Shiva, so he took us all to Marco Island to my brother-in-law Richard's house. We couldn't all stay there, so some of us stayed at the Hilton. One of Richard's friends was the general manager at the Hilton, and owed him a favor. That favor turned out well for us as we were given the Presidential suite. It was a gorgeous two-bedroom suite, with a living room and dining room, on the top floor of the hotel.

My father-in-law stayed in Richard's son's room at his house. While we were at Richard's house one day, the adults were all sitting around the living room talking, and two of my kids (Sarah age 10 and Jeff age 6) were in Richard's son's room playing. They found a toy gun, or so they thought. However, since my father-in-law was staying in that room, it was not a toy gun at all, but a REAL 357 Magnum. All I know is that one shot was fired, and we all went running. Thank God, the gun was fired into the floor and not pointed at anyone. The kids had no idea that it was real since they were in their cousin's room, who was also just a kid. We were all pretty shaken by what happened. To this day, I truly believe my mother-in-law was looking after them.

The next time a higher power intervened was when we were going to a beach vacation in Jupiter. Melissa had just received her driver's license. She wanted to have a car there, so that she and the girls from the other family we were meeting could go out if they wanted too. We agreed, and she followed us in her car with Jeff and Sarah. We got half way there, and it started to rain.

There was an area of road on the turnpike that had just been widened, but it didn't have the final surface on it. As I looked in my rear view mirror, Melissa's car started to hydroplane, and then it spun out of control. She crossed a lane of active traffic, just missing a tractor trailer, and then she crossed into two expanded lanes that were not yet open, coming to rest just feet from the middle barrier.

As I stopped the car in those unopened lanes and put the car in reverse to get back to them, Joy opened the car door, to run to them. I grabbed her and said, "Stay in the car. We'll get to them faster in reverse." They were very shaken, but not a scratch on them or the car–unbelievable. Again, I say my mother-in-law, or God, or both were watching after them that day. We continued the trip with me driving one car, and Joy driving the other.

Regrets

You should never look back, but given the ability to play Monday morning quarterback in print, I would only change a few things. First, I think Joy and I would both agree that we should have stayed fit and active our whole lives. We were sedentary for a number of years, until a cruise on the Queen Mary II. We looked around at all the wheelchairs and oxygen tanks, and said, "This is not going to be us." Today we do Orange Theory Fitness (interval and weight training) to stay fit.

Second, is that we would have also passed this concept down to the kids. Third, we should have eaten healthier while the kids were growing up. As my adult kids constantly point out, the healthier food served in the house when they come over for Sunday night dinner is much better than it was when they were growing up.

Random Thoughts

Rereading this chapter, I had a number of other thoughts about the kids to convey, so here they are in really random fashion:

Lenny & Edith

As I've clearly written about my differences with my father, he was just the opposite with my kids. He was a doting grandfather. Whenever any of the kids were restless in a restaurant, he was the first to pick them up and hold them, or take them outside and play with them until they were ready to come back–ignoring the fact that his food would undoubtedly be cold when he returned.

Edith, while not as doting, always had stuff at the house for them to play with, and she always had some of their favorite food. She specially made Jell-O, with and without bananas, Mandel bread, and ice cream. We would go over to their house in Miami Beach almost every weekend, or while my dad could still drive, they'd come to us.

Beverly & Bill

Joy's parents were just as caring about our kids, even though they already had five other grandchildren. We would enjoy Sunday afternoons at their house in the pool, with all of Joy's siblings and their kids. Her father would do the cooking; he was a great cook.

They had Chihuahuas. Some were friendly, some not so friendly. On occasion you'd have to flick one of them off your ankle as they bit you. Ok, it was a light flick (I don't want to get the animal activists after me).

I think it was a result of visiting both sets of grandparents, while the kids were growing up, combined with how our kids were brought up, that explains why they all return with the grandkids and granddogs every Sunday, either for dinner or brunch. Yes, they bring their dogs. So it's our three kids, two spouses, sometimes a girlfriend, two grandkids, and a total of four dogs and one cat, running around the house. Nothing but bedlam for several hours. It's great!

Papa Lenny and Jeff

Edith, Beverly and Jeff

Papa Lenny and Melissa

Religion

Joy and I, while growing up Jewish, have never been very religious. Yes, we've gone to High Holiday Services, celebrate Hanukah and Passover, but that's about it.

When the kids were young, they attended Sunday Hebrew School and then studied Hebrew so they could get Bar/Bat Mitzvah'd. They were all Bar/Bat Mitzvah'd with big parties held to celebrate the event of them becoming men and women in the eyes of Judaism. I wouldn't change any of it because they are such good memories, but it did put us in the poor house for awhile. The amount of money spent on the parties was like throwing a wedding.

Speaking of weddings, Melissa and John decided that both their religions were important to them, so we hired a rabbi and a priest to perform their ceremony. A year later, I guess, it wasn't so important anymore to Melissa, as she announced, much to our surprise, that she was converting to Catholicism. Given a choice, to disown our daughter or to suck it up, after about a week, we decided to suck it up.

When you really think about it, unless you're a religious zealot –sorry, but all religions have their share of them – it just boils down to what your beliefs are. Most of the time, it's what you're born into and taught. Sometimes people change as they grow, and as individuals they are looking for something different. And that's okay.

Sarah's wedding was a much smaller affair. It was just immediate family and a few of her and Corey's friends. A Jedi Rabbi Minister married them on the beach. Yes, my son-in-law, John, got ordained online as a Jedi Minister and married them. I think it's a legal marriage.

Melissa and John in 2009

Sarah and Corey in 2013

Wilma

It was October 2005, and it was our 25th wedding anniversary. I booked a weekend cruise and unknown to Joy, I invited our good friends from Tampa, Gene and Laura, to join us. As we prepared to leave, Hurricane Wilma, a category one storm, was hitting Mexico's Yucatan Peninsula and was predicted to turn towards South Florida.

While Joy thought I was crazy for insisting we take the cruise, I boarded up the house, leaving the kids, and off we went. When we got to the port, they again told us we didn't have to go under the circumstances and that we would get a full refund. I conferred with Gene by phone and decided to proceed. Joy was so mad because all the while she thought I was on the phone with work.

Once on board, Gene and Laura snuck up behind Joy and covered her eyes and said, "Guess who?" in a disguised voice. When she turned around, my insistence on taking the cruise made total sense to her. We had a fantastic weekend and cruise—until Monday, the day we were supposed to be back in port.

On Saturday, while still in Nassau, I called home and found out Wilma was coming, and it was going to be a Category two hurricane when it hit. Given that information, I had the kids go to Miami and pick up my mother and bring her back to the house. She could not be by herself in a hurricane.

When Wilma hit on Monday, the house, kids and Grandma were secure. The house took a pounding and ultimately we ended up with a new roof, as we lost many roof tiles. Joy, Gene, Laura and I rode out the storm on the ship, zig zagging between the Bahama Islands with hurricane force winds in 15 to 20-foot seas. There were many seasick people on the ship, Joy included. Joy spent the day in the cabin, and Gene, Laura and I continued to enjoy ourselves. About midnight we called it quits when the seas became 25-30 feet. It was time to go to bed...and hang on.

The next morning we were back in port at Cape Canaveral picking up supplies and heading home to "save the troops." We had no electricity, along with 3.4 million others. Since I worked for the power company, I went right to work and was pretty much gone from home for three weeks.

We shipped my mother off to my brother in Jacksonville, as it was not safe for her to be in a dark, powerless house. Funny thing is, the power came back on right after she left. It was still best for her and for us.

All in all everyone survived, and we have the memories of that weekend.

Work – Successes, Disappointments, and Dead Bodies

The very first thing you should know about me and work is that while I've had a successful career–work does not define me. Each time I've changed positions and worked with new people, I've made it very clear that my philosophy was that we needed to enjoy what we did, enjoy the relationships we make, and that it's only a job–a means to an end if you will–to support the rest of our lives. It can't be all consuming, and it has to be balanced. That said, I still have some stories to tell from a not-too-dull accounting career.

The Big 8

When I started in public accounting there were the "Big 8" accounting firms, and then everyone else. I worked for the tenth largest CPA firm called Grant Thornton. Grant had a lot of significance for me as it formed the basis of my career, and it's where I met my wife. It showed me what I didn't want to do: audit, and what I wanted to do: management consulting, or to leave public accounting altogether and move to the corporate accounting world.

Spending four years there, I worked in audit for only one year. Then I worked in management consulting for the remaining three years. I enjoyed the different assignments and working more directly with corporate management on issues they really wanted solved. It was fulfilling. I seem to recall my son saying to me on one of those "take your kid to work days," that "I'll never do what you do."

Funny now, as he's doing exactly that. A CPA in "Big 4" (consolidation of the former Big 8), he worked audit for two years, couldn't stand it, and he is now in consulting. Imagine that. Just like the Harry Chapin song, "Cat's in the Cradle" says, "He's grown up just like me...my boy is just like me."

One of the clients I worked for was AIMEE. I can't remember what it stood for, but they were based in Atlanta. They owned strip coal mines in Alabama, underground coal mines in Tennessee, oil wells in Oklahoma, and a bridge construction company in Florida.

I flew all over the country on that assignment, and on one of those flights I was on their corporate plane, and I had a revelation. They only used one pilot back then, and I thought, what if this old guy (probably 45) flying the plane has a heart attack. I'm dead because I can't fly. Needless to say, after that I always tried to fly commercial.

That job led to another for the same group where I set up the books for a horse farm in Kentucky. However, that's just the lead into the real story. All of those companies were developed by the principles of ESM Government Securities. While I never worked on the ESM account, the proverbial shit hit the fan about three years after I left Grant. It turned out ESM was a Ponzi scheme that blew up in 1985. By Enron and Bernie Madoff standards, it was small potatoes, $300 million. However, it caused the temporary closure of 70 Savings and Loans in Ohio, cost a few accountants their livelihood, and had a Grant Thornton partner, who I worked for and respected, convicted of fraud and sentenced to nine years in jail.

Even though I had already left Grant, I felt like I was in the middle of it. That's because my wife was also that partner's Administrative Assistant. As a result, we were living the case while she was pregnant with our second child. Joy was subpoenaed to testify before the Securities and Exchange Commission at seven months pregnant. Lucky for us, the partner settled with the SEC, and just like that, it was over.

Community News

When I left Grant Thornton, I went to work for my brother-in-law in the newspaper business he had bought from his father (or so I thought). Let me start out by saying NEVER WORK FOR FAMILY.

There were IRS issues, cash flow issues, and serious personnel issues. I think I was there about four months when I received a sign from God to move on. Since the shop was not in the best of neighborhoods, we had an old security guard (and I'm using that term very loosely), who watched over the place at night. Most nights he just threw an old mattress down and slept anywhere he wanted.

That fateful (there is that word again) morning, I came to work only to discover him dead. He had thrown his mattress down between my desk and my credenza, laid down to sleep, and died. Yup, a dead body in my office. I was gone as soon as I found another job.

JARTRAN

James A. Ryder Transportation was the next stop for me. After about four years and two Chapter 11 reorganizations, I bailed for a more stable company, leaving just before JARTRAN went out of business.

I made some life-long friends in Jose and Mike, both of whom I followed to the next company. At JARTRAN I used to run a large processing shop of about 90 people, who processed contracts and paid dealers their commission. Only two days stand out in my mind from those days, and they stand in stark contrast – one funny and one very sad. Funny: a group of data entry clerks that worked for me would key in 200,000 contracts a month. They would also listen to soap operas while they were doing the work, as it was all hand-eye coordination, no thinking was involved. Well, the day Jenny died on All My Children, all work stopped, and there was so much crying over a dumb soap opera.

Sad: January 28, 1986, one month before I left the company, the space shuttle Challenger exploded 73 seconds after liftoff. No work got done that day either, but that was completely understandable.

FPL

I got to Florida Power & Light on pure chance, yet again. I had interviewed for a job that I didn't want in their Accounting Research Department, but figured I could use the experience interviewing. I didn't get that job, but someone I spoke with that day remembered me for another job a month later: Manager of Consolidations with the newly-formed parent company, FPL Group. That job I got, and to this day, 30 years later, I still have my original offer letter.

Make no mistake about it, FPL has been very good to me and my family over the years. I have had many jobs there, each with more responsibility, and I have worked a number of different disciplines that you would not normally think was an accountant's role. The company has great people, and I've made relationships that will last a lifetime. I've made it through a number of reorganizations or downsizings, only to come out on the other end better for it. The company has allowed me so many moves over my career, which has made it interesting and different enough to spend a career at one company, which I know is unusual these days.

Through the years, until his retirement in 2010, I had a fantastic mentor in the Vice President of Accounting/Controller. Mike helped teach me and mold me into the leader I am today. Joy and I still see Mike and his wife, Sandy, socially a few times a year, and we catch up on trips, family, and sometimes even a little advice for the office.

All that said, there comes a time when you stop going up the corporate ladder. That realization for me was tough to take at first. But now I see my role as mentoring the next generation of leaders at FPL, trying to impart to them my philosophy of relationship building and work/life balance.

Some of the more interesting assignments I've had, either from the work or the people aspect of the job, included things like running Payroll and Accounts Payable in the early 1990's. We worked through re-engineering the department, taking it from 85 to 26 people, putting in new systems, offering direct deposit and electronic data interchange (EDI) for the first time. We also created positive pay (sending of a file to the bank of the daily cut checks). This greatly reduced our exposure to check fraud.

Also during that time we experienced Hurricane Andrew. It was a devastating storm that jogged 50 miles to the south at the last minute, sparing Broward County and most of Dade County. The destruction was mostly in South Dade County where FPL had to replace the entire electrical infrastructure. In 1992 most employees were not on direct deposit, and the ATMs were very early versions of what we have today, most of which didn't work anyway without power. I had the great task of getting money to employees. Doing so meant flying in helicopters all over the county to bring the money to the various sites.

I distributed $1.7 million **in cash**, given as advances to employees. Flying over South Dade in a helicopter, I was one of the first people into Turkey Point Nuclear Plant. I flew into the

Working hurricane restoration after Hurricane Charley in Daytona Beach 2004

plant so that employees, who rode out the storm, would have some money to look after their families. One time we landed at Cutler Plant, and two things happened as we landed. First, we blew dirt over everyone eating lunch, and they had to get new lunches. (They were not happy campers, but they felt better when we handed them the money.)

Two, I found a $20 bill on the ground as we landed, and I thought my bag of money had a hole in it, and I was waiting for the rest to come flying out. But it was just a random $20 that Hurricane Andrew left for me to find. In going though that large amount of money, the bank actually let a $50 Silver Certificate slip through. I snagged that puppy, replacing it with a couple of regular $20s and a $10. I still have it to this day.

After Payroll, I worked for two years as Internal Audit Manager, working for a lady named Maria. She knew how to lead, motivate, innovate, and deliver quality products. I learned a lot from her. From there I spent two years as Human Resources System Manager, re-engineering processes and moving Payroll from Accounting, into Human Resources, no small feat. Our Controller was just that controlling, and thought it was a bad idea to let the "touchy feely" guys in HR run one of the most important and costly areas the company had. In the end, it went fine, and that job was a stepping stone into one of the more different roles for an accountant: leading the Y2K project for the entire company and its affiliates.

Y2K had a lot of paranoia surrounding it. With all the hard

Published in the Miami New Times: "FPL's Sol Stamm strikes a confident pose. There will be power on January 1."

work done around the world by IT professionals, it became a non-event. But leading up to the event, it was a large-project management job, with millions of lines of code and thousands of embedded chips to check. We rolled power plants forward into the year 2000, six months ahead of time, just to make sure that we had no issues. I gave numerous TV interviews and participated in viewer call-in talk shows and panel discussions with the likes of the Florida Lt. Governor and President Clinton's Y2K Czar, John Kaskinen.

It was an interesting job to say the least, with a bunch of great people that I'm glad to say are still friends today. All except one. We lost Miguel to cancer several years ago. He was such a smart and kind soul. We were all truly affected by him as we all try daily to emulate his kind nature and ability to get work done at the same time. He is missed by many.

After Y2K, life took a unpredictable turn as I went to work as Controller of FiberNet, an FPL Group subsidiary in the fiber optics business. The work was not unpredictable—it was a lot of fun creating a business from scratch. "Unpredictable" was our president. The man was a bit moody and "eccentric" to put it mildly.

I'm not even sure where to begin on, as I call them, stories of the president. Let me start by saying that the first of his direct reports, of which I was one, to have contact with him in the morning would call the others. This was to let us all know what kind of mood we would be dealing with that day. And, taking the words from *Forrest Gump*, each day was "like a box of chocolates," you never knew what you were going to get.

Besides the difficulty in starting a company and the camaraderie that it brings, here are a few of the more bazar FiberNet stories from that time.

Hearts

The president would have his direct report staff meetings once a week. In this one particular meeting, he was badgering me on depreciation of certain equipment. I told him what my decision was and that if he wanted to check that my answer was right, we could call the Accounting Research Group together for a final answer. He went on and on with his own depreciation theory for another ten minutes. Finally I said to him, "Get off it and move on, and we'll make the call after the meeting." He moved on, but about ten minutes later I looked over to his pad of paper, and he was drawing hearts with my name in the middle of each heart.

Fire Drill

Fire drills in the General Office building were a twice a year occurence. On this day we were in the president's office when one struck. We had to walk down from the sixth floor to the parking lot. When we were passing the fifth floor, a blind worker from FPL got ahead of us, and of course, he was being led, and they were taking their time to be safe. We got out of the building, and out of ear shot of the employee, and the president says, "If this had been a real fire, he would have had footprints going up his back as I walked over him."

Grain of Salt

The president used to beat up the sales force on their sales techniques, and I would agree some of them needed it and deserved it. This one day he asked this sales guy, "Didn't I tell you to do this...or that?"

The salesman said, "Yes, but sometimes I take what you say with a grain of salt." Wrong answer.

The president called me the next morning on my way into the office, and he was sounding so proud of himself, so I said, "What's up?"

He said, "I fixed that sales guy with the grain of salt comment."

I said, "Really, what did you do."

He said, "I took ten pounds of salt and covered his desk with it."

He was laughing hysterically; I was appalled. Then all of a sudden the laughing stopped, and he realized that we had just had an anthrax scare in the building a few weeks earlier, and asked me if I thought that someone might think it was anthrax. I think he high-tailed it into the guy's office and cleaned it up before anyone saw it.

Let's go to the Parking Lot ~ I'll Kick Your Ass

It wasn't always the president. We had this engineering manager with a bit of a Napoleon complex. He and I butted heads on a number of occasions, as I was responsible for controls in the business, and he just wanted to construct network with little checks and balances. One time after a heated conversation on the phone, he hung up abruptly and showed up in my office about a minute later, fists raised and wanting to go to the parking lot and kick my ass. He was about a foot and a half shorter and at least 75 pounds lighter than me. I suggested to him that he might want to back off and get the f#$% out of my office before he got hurt, or I filed a complaint with HR, whichever I felt like doing. He left, and not another word was said to anyone about it.

Pigeons

The last story is about a Caucasian Controller, me, and an African American, Vice President of Sales. We had a great working relationship and a friendship. We were in the president's office this fine morning on the sixth floor of the building, which had a balcony on it. It was not a usable space, as you couldn't get out since there were no doors. While we were meeting, these two pigeons, a white one and a black one, flew onto the balcony and starting the mating dance that turned into...well let's just say they were intimate.

The president turned to us and said, "Look, the black guy jumped the honky and is having his way with her." The Sales VP and I just looked at each other as if to say, "Did he really just say that?" We could barely contain ourselves. Once the meeting was over, we left his office and headed down the stairwell to our offices on the fifth floor. We didn't get halfway there when we both just about pissed our pants, as we were laughing so hard at what had just been said and how inappropriate the comment was. We both used to tell each other that we needed to write these stories down and publish them someday.

To sum it up, FiberNet was a lot of fun, even though the president did put us through the ringer and caused us almost as much pain as laughter.

I then left FiberNet and went back to work at FPL, as Director of Corporate Planning. In that role, I worked directly for the President of FPL and the CFO of FPL. It was more of a strategic role, that allowed me the opportunity to gain exposure to the whole company.

After a couple of years, I was asked to take on the role of Fleet Nuclear Controller. This position covered two companies and five nuclear power stations, with eight nuclear generating units spread out around the country. It was a very stressful, but rewarding time. It's fun working in the operations world where things are happening real time and decisions have to be made on a daily basis.

Nuclear is unlike any other type of business and is actually a business within a business. There IS no margin for error, and safety is first above all else. The business side of the house was secondary, after operating the plants. As such, it was challenging and stressful to manage the budget.

After five years, I felt it was time for a change, a job with a little less stress. It seemed like the right decision at the time, but it turned out to be the wrong decision. I ended up in a staff role, far from operations and was bored quickly. It was probably the first misstep of my career. Needless to say, other than my staff, which I absolutely loved and who made the job somewhat bearable, it was not a good fit for me.

I've been able to move on from the staff role, and have now gone back to an operational support role in FPL's Power Delivery Business Unit (poles & wires). It's new, and I'm learning. At a minimum, it will be interesting, and fun for the remainder of my time with the company, and I'm appreciative of the opportunity.

In what could be my final position in the company, besides fulfilling my responsibilities, the mentoring role has become even more of a focus for me. It's a way to impact the organization for years to come, and it provides me with additional satisfaction.

I'm hoping to finish my career at FPL in another three to

five years, which will provide me the opportunity to retire in a financially sound position.

That said, given an opportunity when I'm done at FPL, I really don't want to retire. What I'd actually like is to pursue a second career away from accounting/finance and towards the travel industry, specifically the cruise industry. This statement should come as no surprise to those who know me. Looking back and accumulating all of the cruises I've been on, a total of 44 as of January 2016, I've spent almost a full year of my life cruising. I suppose this should qualify me for some sort of role within the industry.

Globetrotters

Over the years I've lost a number of co-workers and friends to untimely early deaths from cancer and heart attacks. In 2005, the loss of two particular coworkers had a profound impact on my life and that of the rest of the family.

One died of a heart attack in his sleep. He was 48 and in great shape, training for a Disney half marathon. In fact, he was in my office the day before he died, and I still remember that we talked about some business issues, and then family. The next morning when I got a call on my way into work that he'd passed away in his sleep, I actually heard the name, but didn't connect it to him for about ten seconds. I guess the thought of him passing away was just so foreign, my brain didn't process it fast enough.

The second death was from colon cancer. Again, it was a co-worker, who complained about a stomachache and went to the emergency room, only to get the cancer diagnosis. He died a few agonizing months later.

These events, along with my in-laws passing away at the early age of 70, while still working, really changed my perspective on life. None of these people got to enjoy the so called "golden years." It made me think that you need to enjoy yourself while you can, since (as the old saying goes) we don't know what tomorrow will bring. We don't know if we'll even get to our golden years of retirement, or whether we'll even be in good enough health to enjoy them.

With this epiphany, Joy and I set out to make as many memories as we could with the kids, and now the grandkids. We have traveled parts of the globe and plan to do more and see more as we stay active, not waiting for retirement. In a newspaper article I once read about author Dianne Hales, she said the following, which I believe really sums up my thoughts on what I want for my family. She said, "There is a quote from St. Augustine that not traveling is the equivalent of reading only a single page in an immense book. From an early age, I wanted more and more pages, to see new things, hear new sounds, taste new foods, experience new adventures. Travel adds so many dimensions, colors, memories, perspectives, feelings."

We've traveled to many countries, not just to sightsee, but to learn about the local culture and the people who live there. We have had many wonderful experiences and met many wonderful people along the way. Most of the travel has been by ship to allow us the opportunity to experience as much as possible, getting a taste for an area so that we could plan to go back by land and stay longer in the places that seemed special to us.

We've traveled to England, Ireland, Scotland, France, Norway, Sweden, Finland, Russia, Estonia, Demark, Netherlands, Spain, Italy, Greece, Turkey, Croatia, Portugal, Azores, Canada, Mexico, Belize, Panama, Aruba, Bonaire, Barbados, Granada, Dominica, US Virgin Islands, St. Maarten, Antigua, Turks and Caicos, Jamaica, the Caymans, and the Bahamas. A nice list, but one that I hope will continue to grow.

In all of these countries we've had some fantastic guides willing to share their culture. We have gone back to a number of places many times and have favorite restaurants we visit again and again.

On one of our past favorite trips, we traveled throughout Italy for 12 days with our good friends, Lynn and Bob. We stayed in a 12th century castle, an Agriturismo (working farm), a B&B,

and a room by the sea. We flew into Rome and drove to Perugia, Siena, Florence, Cinque Terre, Parma and Milan. We stopped in many small towns like Orvieto and Assisi, meeting the locals and creating memories that will last forever. We ate, drank (a lot), learned to cook an Italian meal, and watched a small local company make Parmigianino Reggiano wheels from scratch. We met friends from a previous cruise, who live in Perugia, and drank some more. From there we flew to Paris for a few days, going to

Me, Bob, Lynn, Andrea, Joy
Spello, Italy, 2010

Cooking Class in
Florence, Italy, 2010

Champaigne Tasting in Epernay,
France in 2010

Gondola ride in Venice, Italy,
2014

Giverny (Monet's house and gardens) and to Epernay to see Moet & Chandon's Champagne facilities and of course, Champagne tasting.

On another trip with Lynn and Bob, we took a Baltics cruise. We brought Jeff and Sarah, and they brought their daughter, Amanda. It was a great vacation, experiencing cultures from England to Denmark, Norway, Sweden, Finland, Estonia, and Russia.

In Russia, we took a shore excursion from St. Petersburg to Moscow, which involved planes, trains, buses and automobiles. We left the ship at 6:30 a.m. and returned at 1 a.m. St. Petersburg to Moscow involved an hour and a half flight on a Russian made plane, which was quite the experience. Armed military guards met us at the airport and the plane. Jeff was separated out for questioning and frisked. No pictures were allowed of the plane, and anyone who tried, got their camera confiscated. Realizing we were "not in Kansas anymore," we all complied for the day.

The plane itself was a throwback to the early 70's. It was a wide body, like an old Lockheed L1011. We walked up through the belly of the plane, through the luggage compartment, to get to the cabin. Rather than air blowing from a vent above, each seatback had a fan spinning. The tires on this plane 'were way past old'. Bob and I noticed them when we got on. I have never seen Bob sweat so much, and by the time we landed, he was drenched.

Sarah, who is not a good flyer by any stretch of the imagination, actually fell asleep. She awoke freaked out, thinking we were about to crash. The reason was the alarm the plane made when the pilots put the fasten seatbelt sign on. Instead of the simple ping you hear on almost all of today's airliners, this plane set off a siren that blared from speakers somewhere on the plane. It was very startling, to say the least.

In the end, it was a fantastic day and a little surreal being in Red Square, seeing Lenin's tomb, and touring the inside of the Kremlin where all the czars are encrypted.

The next day in St. Petersburg, we toured the Hermitage Museum, which is an absolutely unbelievable site. It holds works from Michael Angelo, Leonardo Da Vinci, Rembrandt, Degas, Picasso, Monet, Chagall, Dali and the list goes on and on. It has more artwork than the Louvre Museum in Paris. What struck us as odd is how close you can get to all the artwork, and the fact that on this cold and rainy day the windows were open, exposing the artwork to the elements. Shameful. Both Jeff and Sarah appreciated the magnitude of what they were seeing. Even Jeff, at 15 years old, commented and asked, "Why don't they take care of the artwork better?" My response was, "Lack of money." His comeback was, "All they'd have to do is sell one or two pieces."

Red Square, Moscow 2006

St. Petersburg, Russia 2006

We have taken our kids all over the world with us and have some great experiences and memories to look back on. For the most part, the trips were without incident, although Sarah, before she got married and had a child, was quite the personality to travel with. We were laughing one Sunday night at dinner, as I recounted how many different countries and cities Sarah "flipped me off." From London to Rome to Moscow, I got "the finger" for one reason or another.

On another trip, Jeff was 18, and he talked me into letting him drink beer and wine on the cruise. I signed a paper allowing the cruise line to serve him. Little did I know, he would make friends with a bartender, who would serve him liquor for free.

It was three in the morning when the phone rang. It was Melissa and Sarah summoning my wife to Sarah's and Jeff's cabin. Apparently, Jeff, having had too much to drink, was singing in Hebrew, Spanish and English and had proceeded to vomit all over the bedding, carpet and curtains. SO even though in Spanish, he said to the girls, "No Padre, no Madre," my wife was called to the rescue. Jeff never saw Dublin the next day. He slept it off in our cabin while the ship cleaned his cabin and replaced the bedding and curtains.

Traveling really gives you the opportunity to meet people from all over. We have friends that live in Italy and the U.S. that we might never have met without Joy's insistence and ignoring my preference. We met Andrea and Ester in Croatia sitting by a stream eating lunch.

I had wanted to sit with some Americans to have decent conversation, and Joy wanted to sit by the stream. Only problem was that the people sitting by the stream were speaking Italian, and we couldn't converse. Well, as it turned out, they spoke perfect English, and we had a wonderful time with them. Andrea later introduced us to his brother, Adriano and his wife, Laura, whom we have been friends with ever since. We have had many dinners together as they live close by in Miami. A small world...

As I said, traveling opens up the mind to other cultures and possibilities. As long as Joy and I can physically do it, we will travel.

St. Thomas Harbor - 2014

Dunns River Falls, Jamaica - 1995

Maegan's Bay, St. Thomas - 2014

Zip lining in St. Maarten - 2008

Sea Kayaking, Northern California, 2011

Wine Tasting, Napa Valley, 2011

Santorini, Greece, 2014

Exploring Glacier, Alaska, 2009

Manarola, Cinque Terra, Italy, 2010

The Search, The Letter, The Crazy Week

Mindset on Searching for my Birth Family

State of Mind

Even though I knew I was adopted from an early age, searching for my birth parents really didn't cross my mind. I knew who my parents were...Lenny & Edith Stamm. I was comfortable with that. Funny thing is that I told people throughout the years that I was adopted. I even told Joy on our first date. However, the topic NEVER came up at home, and I NEVER had even the first conversation about it with my adopted brother. I can't tell you why, only that we never talked about it.

While I was in my twenties, I did think about being adopted from time to time and what it meant. I assumed that I was the product of a teenage pregnancy, and since I was born in the mid 1950's, I thought the stigma of being a single mother made my birth mother give me up for adoption. I thought about the potential that she eventually married, and that I might have a half-brother or sister somewhere out there.

Truth be told, I also thought that I might have been the product of a rape, an unwanted memory, an unwanted child. The thought of that scared me enough, combined with the good life I had, to never look further than my own thoughts.

As I've said before, my son Jeff considers me 'risk adverse', so I think the shoe fit in this instance as well...as in don't rock the boat...life is good.

Maturing and the Half-Hearted search for Medical History

As life went on, I was well established, in my forties, with a good job, and married. I had kids going to college, and I was very comfortable in my own skin.

The year was 2002, and my cousin, Barbara, for some reason out of the blue, sent me an article that was in the Philadelphia Inquirer about adoption and ways to find your birth parents. I can't remember who the article was about, but for some reason it spurred me into action.

I sent two letters as the article suggested—one to the Pennsylvania Department of Health looking for birth information prior to my adoption, and one to the Adoption Medical History Registry in Pennsylvania.

At this point in my life, I had had a couple of medical issues, mainly with high blood pressure (weight-related) and numerous eye issues (detached retinas, etc). I was really only searching for medical records, with little interest in actually finding my birth parents.

Both requests turned up nothing. The State basically told me they could only release identifying records if a biological parent filed a Biological Parent Registration Identification Form with the Division of Vital Records. They had not.

The Registry also informed me that my biological parents were not in the registry, but they would keep my request on file in case they ever registered. With that news in April 2003, my search came to an end.

Searching for Blue Eyes

On February 9, 2011, my second grandson was born. Although I didn't know it, that would be the start of a new search, nine years later.

John Thomas was born with blue eyes and blonde hair. None of us had those hereditary traits. We all had dark hair and brown eyes. As time went on, his eye color stayed blue, not changing as many infants do over time.

As he approached 18 months old, Melissa and John looked up the genealogy behind where John Thomas' blue eyes came from. They promptly laid the origin right down to me. It could only come from the grandfather's gene pool. Whether they were right or wrong about that conclusion, it didn't matter. My kids had finally pushed me hard and far enough to attempt to continue my previous half-hearted search, and this time to try to open Pandora's box.

Based on the results of the last failed attempt, I knew two things. One, I wasn't going to tell my kids about the search and get their hopes up. Two, I needed help.

I must have picked up the phone to call a search company named OmniTrace a dozen times only to chicken out and hang up. Finally, in late October 2012, I made contact.

Things moved quickly from that point forward. After signing an agreement with OmniTrace, they provided me with a list of forty questions. They ranged from: what were the ages of my birthparents, to were they married, to was I in a foster home, to the name of the social worker who handled my placement, to medical information on my birth family, and a lot of other questions in-between.

OmniTrace also provided me with the place to send the request to. In my case, it was the Pennsylvania Court of Common Pleas Family Division.

The response came back quickly on November 14, 2012, to be exact. It was somewhat disheartening, as it said my adoption did not occur in Pennsylvania. According to Pennsylvania Vital Records, the location of my final adoption occurred in Dade County, Florida. OmniTrace comforted me by explaining that this happens all the time, and we now just had to send the same request to the State of Florida Department of Children and Families.

On December 11, 2012, I received a letter of acknowledgement from the State of Florida of my request of non-identifying information from my closed adoption record. It also stated that the review could take several months to complete, and they would get back to me once completed.

With that, I put the search out of my mind yet again, thinking nothing would come, and we'd be at another dead end.

The Letter ~ January 14, 2013

It was January 14, 2013. I got home from work around 7 p.m. and went to the mailbox for the mail before walking into the house. I proceeded to toss the mail on the counter and walk away to go change into something more comfortable before dinner. There amongst the bills and other bulk mail items was an envelope from the State of Florida Department of Children and Family Services. Having remembered the last letter saying it would take several months, I thought this was just an update that would say, "We're still working on it." I couldn't be more wrong.

Joy saw the letter as well, and after I had changed and came back to the kitchen/family room, she was in disbelief that I'd just left it on the counter, and that I'd proceeded to open up all the other mail.

She said, "Open the letter."

I said, "I'll get to it." I think part of me was a little scared as to what might be lurking within the envelope.

Once all the other mail was disposed of, I said to Joy, "Let's eat, and I'll open the letter after dinner." She was having none of that and insisted I open it.

I caved in at that point and opened the letter from the State. As we started to read it, we soon discovered that this was what we had been waiting for…actual information.

Joy was reading faster than me, and with each paragraph,

she would start to tell me something about what she just read. I finally stopped her and said, "Keep it to yourself, I'm reading slower than you, and I want to try and take it all in as I read it."

It was an incredible letter. At the same time, it confirmed my worse fears, provided me the knowledge of why I was given up for adoption, and it opened up a whole new world of possibilities. The letter changed my life forever in a way that I couldn't even imagine.

Instead of recounting what it said, here it is in its entirety. In reading it, keep in mind that this letter is very unusual for its detail, but it contains only non-identifying information as the State is required to do. That said, it's really "breadcrumbs" left by my birth mother to help me to understand both why I was given up for adoption, and also to hopefully help me find my way back to the family.

It took a lot for my birth mother to tell her story, a lot for the Pennsylvania social worker in the 1950's to write it all down, and then a lot for the social worker with the State of Florida today to include all of that information in this letter to me—56 years later.

Rick Scott Governor
David E. Wilkins Secretary
January 7, 2013
Mr. Solomon L. Stamm

Dear Mr. Stamm,

I am writing in response to your request for non-identifying information on your birth family from the closed adoption record. Florida law does provide for the release of this type of information to adult adoptees upon written request and with proper proof of identification. Thank you for providing this office with proof of your identity.

I have reviewed the closed adoption record and I have extracted all of the information that I am allowed to release to you under the Florida Adoption Law. If, after you read the information that is presented in this letter, you feel that you are still in need of additional information from the closed adoption record, you will have to secure a court order from the Dade County Circuit Court where your adoption was finalized.

The record documented that you were born on October 22, 1956 in Philadelphia, Philadelphia County, Pennsylvania. The attendant at birth was David Silverman, D.O.

Your birth mother and birth father signed the consents for your adoption plan on March 28, 1957. The document was properly witnessed and notarized. According to the record, your birth mother stated that although your birth father signed the consent, he was not aware he was signing a consent for adoption. He thought, rather, that he was signing a death certificate for the infant. The record stated that your birth mother said he had been drinking at the time and she had folded the paper in such a way that only the place needing a signature was exposed. The record further documents that this issue was reviewed prior to the finalization of the adoption and it was decided that there was legal precedent in Florida to proceed with the adoption.

Your birth mother opposed having the Department interview her husband. She stated that he did not know about the adoption and she was concerned he might reveal that the child was placed for adoption to people in the area and this might give him the opportunity to make trouble for her and her children. According to the record, she further stated that she would consider having the baby returned to her if the interview was necessary. Your birth father's probation officer stated that your birth father was a very irresponsible person who supported his family irregularly and caused the family much anxiety. He also stated that he felt your birth mother had done a good job of raising her children.

According to the record, your birth mother was in her early 40's when you were born. Your birth parents were married in the summer of 1932. They had a stormy, unhappy marriage. Your birth mother said that her husband drank excessively, left her several times and on more than one occasion lived with other women. He failed to support the family for many years. There were nine living children from their marriage in addition to the adoptee. There was one child who died at birth. Shortly before the birth of the tenth child, twelve years prior to your birth, your birth father left his family and your birth parents had been separated since that time.

According to your birth mother, her husband came to her home intoxicated late one night and forced her to have relations with him. You were conceived at that time. Her family physician referred her to Dr. Silverman, who facilitated your adoption with the Stamm's. Your birth mother went to the hospital to deliver you but it was a false alarm. You were expected to be delivered three weeks before you actually were born. The doctors had thought the baby was in a good position, had taken X-rays and had given your birth mother something to induce labor. She went into labor but the labor stopped and the doctors were afraid to let your birth mother go home. A Caesarean section was finally performed as they were afraid to wait any longer.

Your birth mother did not see you or your adoptive parents. She remained in the hospital for nine weeks following your birth. Her husband visited her once following the birth and she told him that the baby had died. The only one in the family who knew about the birth of the child was your birth mother's oldest daughter, Ruth. The rest of the family was told that your birth mother was hospitalized for the removal of a tumor.

The record states that your birth mother presented as a very tense, nervous person who showed she had been under great strain. She stated that she had confidence in Dr. Silverman and felt sure he was making the best possible plan for her child. Your birth mother belonged to the Baptist Church. She stated that she worked for several Jewish families and hoped her child might have a home with the kind people for whom she had worked. She agreed to your placement in a Jewish home.

Your birth mother was steadily employed traying eggs at an egg farm. She earned $44 weekly. Your birth father owned a tractor and was employed irregularly by a trucker, using his own tractor to pull trailers on long trips. Your birth mother did not know where her husband was living at the time of your birth. She received $35 weekly through his probation office after your birth father was ordered to pay child support.

Your birth mother said she had been in good health up to the time of your birth. She said she had been extremely nervous since your birth and expressed concern that her husband's knowledge of the adoption plan would be used by him to influence the other children against her and he would try to reduce the amount of his financial support to her. Your birth mother said that your birth father had suffered from ulcers. She knew of no other serious mental or physical illnesses in the family.

All of your siblings were normal, healthy and intelligent. Your birth mother showed pictures of all of her children. She was obviously proud of them. At the time of your birth, the children were Grover, age 25 and married; Ruth, age 23 and married; Orville, age 22 and married; Allen age 21 and married; Genevieve age 19 and married; Leroy, age 18 and married. At home were Amos, age 16, Janice, age 15 and Dolores, age 12. Three of the older children were purchasing their own homes. There were seven grandchildren.

Your birth mother's parents were both deceased. Your birth mother's mother died of cancer and her father of a heart attack. Your paternal grandparents were both living; your paternal grandfather was 64 years old and your paternal grandmother was 63 years old at the time of your birth. They lived close by and tried to help your birth mother with the children as much as possible. Your paternal grandfather was a hardworking man who worked at the same egg farm as your birth mother. Your birth father was an only child.

This is all of the non-identifying information that is contained in the closed adoption record.

Your adoption by Morris Leonard Stamm and his wife Edith G. Stamm was finalized in the circuit court of Dade County, Florida on October 22, 1957. The Honorable Fritz Gordon was the presiding judge. The Attorney of record was Mr. Schiff from the firm of Dubin, Blatt and Schiff. At the time of your adoption proceeding, Mr. Schiff's office was located at the DuPont Building, Miami, Florida.

Thank you for allowing us to assist. Enclosed with this letter is an application for the Florida Adoption Reunion Registry and the International Soundex Reunion Registry for your information and consideration. If you have any questions about any of the information presented in this letter, or you feel that we may somehow be of any further assistance, please feel free to call me.

Sincerely,

Florida Adoption Reunion Registry Department of Children and Families Office of Family Safety

A Crazy Week Unfolds

The letter arrived and was opened on January 14, 2013, a Monday. I had so many thoughts in my head after reading it and letting it sink it for a bit.

One of my first thoughts was that I wanted to share the information with my cousin, Barbara, who I was closest with, besides my mother and brother, but both of whom I could not share the information with for different reasons. My mother with her Alzheimer's wouldn't understand anything I'd say to her, and my brother who didn't know I was searching, and who gets upset at just the mention of adoption.

It was about 8 p.m. by the time I picked up the phone to call Barbara. Barbara's daughter, Sally, answered the phone, which was odd to begin with. She has her own family and doesn't live there. Then it got even stranger as Sally began crying when she heard my voice. Sally then proceeded to tell me in very broken words, that her sister Stephie, had passed away of a heart attack earlier in the day. She was 56. Everyone, including me, was devastated.

On the very day I got all this life-changing information, I couldn't share it with the one person closest to me. It was upsetting, but totally understandable. It would take about a month before Barbara and I could talk about it.

Tuesday
As the day began, I left for work prepared to discuss the letter with my contact at OmniTrace. Since Joy leaves later than me for

work, she began some research on her own that was very fruitful.

In the letter, there was a paragraph on how proud my birthmother was of all her children, and she actually named them and gave their ages at the time of my birth.

Armed with that information, Joy began a search of the 1940 census. Since the census is indexed, you could enter a set of names and approximate ages and look for a potential match. Of additional help in the search were the unique names of my siblings as they were not just some common Tom, Dick and Harry.

Joy figured out based on their ages at the time of my birth that the 1940 census should contain Grover, Ruth, Allen, Genevieve and Leroy.

She first searched in Pennsylvania records since I was born in Philadelphia and found nothing. Next, she searched New Jersey with that set of first names and BAM there it was—my birth family staring back at her on the computer screen. Given the breadcrumbs left by my birthmother, it took less than 15 minutes to find the Snyder's of Hunterdon County and the Township of Franklin.

My birthmother's name was Elizabeth (Betty) and my birthfather's name was Orville. How about that as a coincidence, as my adopted mother's best friend was named Elizabeth and also went by Betty.

Joy called me on my way to work to give me all this information. By the time I got to work I had a PDF of the 1940 census in my in-box to see for myself.

Needless to say, my contact and data request of OmniTrace with the information provided by Joy had just changed from a search to a confirmation. They were able to do that within an hour, and they were also struck by how unusually detailed the letter was from the State.

As the day wore on, OmniTrace provided me with obituaries for my mother and father, and my six siblings who had passed away.

They were also able to provide married names for the female siblings along with addresses and phone numbers for the four surviving siblings. All the information that was vital if I was considering contacting the family.

Tuesday Night

During the day Joy and I discussed telling our children of the search and the outcome. We called each of them and asked the girls to come over after dinner without their spouses or our grandchildren, and Jeff was to join us via Facetime.

The speculation began and we had to answer these questions:

"No, neither mom or dad is sick."

"No, we did not win the lotto."

They came over around 7 p.m., and we proceeded to tell them of the search, which they knew nothing about, even though they had been badgering me for years to do it.

That surprise led to shock as I slowly read the letter to them in order to let what they were hearing sink in. I got a lot of expressions as we went through it like, "shut up," "no way," "what the hell," and "unbelievable."

After I read it to them, the girls took the letter and read it for themselves to help it sink in.

Wednesday

A day of action on all fronts. I swear to you, I don't think anyone other than Jeff worked that day.

The girls and my wife all set off on their own searches. I can't even count all the emails and texts I received that day. By 2 p.m. I said, "enough"…please stop, I have work to do." At that point they cut me out, but continued between themselves.

Before I cut myself out of the loop, Melissa had sent me a photo of my mother's tombstone, courtesy of www.findagrave.com, along with the cemetery name and location. Who would even think that such a site even existed? Using Google Earth, I got pictures of all the sibling's homes…too creepy for me. You can see why I cut them all off.

OmniTrace even offered to contact the family on my behalf. While I entertained it for a brief moment, I felt that was not the right thing to do, and that I'd have to do it myself.

Later that evening, Joy and I sat down and thought about how to contact Ruth. We knew she would be the contact, as the letter stated she was the only one who knew about me. However, the concern to us was her age. Joy and I have experienced a wide range of people who are 80. There are bad 80's–like my adopted mother in an assisted living facility with no memory, and there are good 80's–like my cousin, Barbara, full of life and active. So which was Ruth, and how should we contact her?

We decided a phone call out of the blue would most likely shock her, so we settled on a simple letter stating that I may be related, and I wanted to make contact with her if she found it in her heart to do so–Nothing pushy at all.

The following is the actual wording of the letter we sent to Ruth:

I am contacting you because I recently began a search for my birth family. The information that I received leads me to believe that you might be a direct family member.

My adoption record revealed that my birth mother mentioned that only her oldest daughter, Ruth, knew about my birth. According to the information that I have accumulated, it's possible that my birth parents were Elizabeth and Orville Snyder. It also mentioned that there were 10 other siblings, including one that died as an infant.

I want you to know that I have had a very good life. Although I am in good health, the purpose of my search originally was to find any background health information that might be useful to my family. My search revealed much more information than I ever anticipated.

I realized instant contact by a phone call might be overwhelming, so I decided to write you a letter. I contacted you first due to the fact that you might be the only sibling that was aware of my birth. I would appreciate being able to speak with you, as now that I know that I had 10 siblings with the same parents, I would like to know more.

Let me provide some background about myself. I was born October 22, 1956 in a hospital in Philadelphia. I have been married 32 years. I have three children, two daughters age 30 and 27, both married with sons. I also have a son who is 23.

I am hoping that you would find it in your heart to contact me.

Sincerely,
Sol Stamm

Thursday

The letter to Ruth was given to Fedex for delivery the next day. Thursday was just a day to reflect on the week.

Friday

I think between Joy and myself we might have worn out Fedex's package tracking system. I even looked at Ruth's house using Google Earth, to imagine if nobody was home where the package would be left. Late morning we received confirmation that the letter had been delivered. Now all we could do was wait. Well that's not exactly true, since I had Ruth's phone number and could call her at any time. I think Joy and I had discussed a three or four day waiting period until I reached out by phone if I didn't hear back.

What I didn't know is that my mother had sworn Ruth to never tell anyone about me, a promise she had held until that Friday. While I think her husband, Walt, knew, her children did not. They've since told me that they always knew if they confided in her about anything, their secret was safe. But even they didn't know how far she would take it.

That afternoon her grandson, James, came by, and she was smiling from ear to ear. James asked her why she was so happy, and she said, "I found my brother." Later that night she let her daughters in on it and enlisted her daughter, Eva, to assist her with a call to me.

Saturday

The day went by without any contact, which had me wondering if my contact was welcomed, or would it be ignored or rebuffed.

Joy and I have season tickets to the Florida Panthers hockey team, and that evening we had a game to attend. As coincidence would have it, it was against the New Jersey Devils. Off we went. In between the first and second periods, I checked my phone for emails and saw that I had a missed call with a New Jersey area code. It was Ruth. No message was left, and at that point it was too late to call back. I do remember showing the phone and commenting to Joy and also to a doctor who sits next to me at the hockey games, "That was a call that was 56 years in the making." I then proceeded to explain the happenings of the week to the doctor.

Sunday

Late Sunday morning I returned the call, but I received voicemail and left a message. It was mid-afternoon when Ruth and Eva returned my call. We spoke for about 45 minutes, during which I recounted several passages from the letter I received from the State. Ruth told me of the hard life they had growing up and the circumstances of my adoption.

She was so happy to finally find me, and she called me her brother. As we said our good-byes and made plans for the next call, as well as an eventual trip to meet, she told me she loved me. I have to admit that took me by surprise and was a bit weird. However, it made me feel very welcome, wanted, and with that the connection was made.

Adoption and My Brother Warren

Before going any further with my discovery of my birth family, I really should talk about my adopted brother, giving some background to understand his reaction to all of this.

Growing up, as I've already established, Warren and I were very different. You might say we came from different gene pools. I was very straight and serious, more the tactical thinker. He was an actor, who then turned into a lawyer, I guess that's sort of one in the same. We were also almost four years apart in age. All of these differences led to us not being very close growing up.

This sort of preamble is for what's about to come next. Since we weren't close, we never even talked about adoption. My adopted parents never talked about it, and I always assumed he knew we were both adopted, so it was never discussed.

In 1999, Joy, Jeff and I went on an Alaskan cruise with my brother, his wife and his kids. This was really the first time we vacationed together. Somewhat strange considering I was mid-forties and he was approximately 40, but again we really weren't that close. We had a great time on that vacation. One night at dinner the conversation turned a little strange for my family as he mentioned that one of his sons had webbed toes like "our father," in a manner that suggested he was in his gene pool. Jeff and Joy looked at me, and I kicked Jeff under the table to keep quiet. You see I figured out, or at least I thought in that moment, that he somehow didn't know he was adopted.

A couple of years passed and my adopted mother was coming

back from Vegas to visit her best friend Betty, and I wanted to ask her about my adoption while I had her alone. Not really knowing that Warren didn't know (I had forgotten about our Alaska experience), I began to tell him, while on my cellphone on my way home from work, of my plans to talk to our mother.

He said, "What are you talking about…adoption?"

My response was, "Hey, I'm getting to a dead zone on cell coverage, and I'll call you back when I get home."

I had to get off the phone with him, as that was the first moment I truly knew he did not know we were both adopted.

I also knew his next question was going to be, "Was I adopted?" While I was 99.9 percent sure that he was, I needed to confirm it. I called my cousin Barbara, and she said, "Of course, he was." Later that night I called him back. We talked for a while, and he asked that question, "what about me?" He was absolutely devastated at age 42 to learn that he was adopted. I felt horrible, but could do nothing to change the facts.

We've had a few more discussions about it, and anytime I even use the word "adoption," he gets upset. He feels like he was lied to his whole life. At one point when he and Denise were just married, someone at the Seasons Apartment House, who knew Warren and knew the doctor's wife who delivered me in Philadelphia, actually said something to them, but they blew it off as just an old lady, who didn't know what she was talking about.

A few months after I told him he was adopted, he called from a Las Vegas bank parking lot. He had excused himself from inside the bank where he was with our adopted parents opening a bank safety deposit box, when they asked him the all important question of....mother's maiden name. It just then struck him that although he had answered that question all his life, now with the knowledge that he was adopted, it was a question for which he had no answer at that particular moment. He was upset about it and had to talk to me.

In June of 2003, my father's health began to fail, as he had congestive heart failure. He had lived nine years with only a 15 percent heart function since his heart attack in 1994. My mother was here in Miami Beach visiting Betty when my brother summoned me out to Las Vegas. My father would not go to the hospital, so I needed to fly out to convince him that he needed to go. I could not tell my mother, so as not to upset her on her flight back to Vegas. I put her on a flight and caught one the very next morning.

During his stay in the hospital and subsequent hospice stay, I asked him why he never told my brother about being adopted. He said, "It was the way you reacted, by running out the door and going to a friend's house for the rest of the day, made our decision not to tell Warren." I think I was about eight years old at the time.

I found what he said kind of strange, because I really didn't even remember that incident until he reminded me of it. Rather how I always recalled knowing that I was adopted was from an incident when I was about six. I recall my mother blurting out something about me being adopted one day when I was being particularly bad. It's that memory that sticks in my mind, not the one my father told me about, which I now seem to recall as well.

After my father died and long after my mother came down with Alzheimer's, Warren asked our mother's best friend Betty why she didn't tell him he was adopted. Her response was, "Your mother said we would no longer be friends if I told you."

Warren's Search

After I received my letter from the State of Florida and after that crazy week where I connected with my birth family, I went to Warren's office one night after work to let him in on it. I felt I had to talk to him face to face, just the two of us.

I think he took the news of my find pretty well; after all, it is what it is. He then decided to do the same search. I contacted the person at the State that had signed my letter and asked if she could also do my brother's request. She agreed and provided Warren with a letter that contained all non-identifying information. Unfortunately, his letter was more the normal letter and did not have the detail that was contained in my letter.

He found out his biological parents were both in the military. His father was a lawyer stationed in Miami, and his mother a paralegal. They were not married, were Baptist and originated from a southern Gulf state. That was it.

To go any further, he would now have to turn to OmniTrace, but for now he is not searching any further.

Me (age 5) and Warren

Me (age 8) and Warren (age 4)

The Search, The Letter, The Crazy Week

Warren, Denise, Joy, and Me 2000

Warren, Lenny, Edith, Me in 1971

Me and Warren in 2014

Stamm Family Picture 1999

Parallel Universes Collide

Birth Parents ~ Elizabeth and Orville

No one seems to know how my birthparents met. What I do know is that they were married in 1932 and proceeded to have eleven children.

Their marriage had many ups and downs, as he was both an alcoholic and a womanizer. Even Ruth said, the first time we spoke, what a bad man our father was. They seemed to be total opposites as a couple.

My birth father worked sporadically, and the family moved from relative to relative, having no money for a place of their own. He left the family many times to live with other women, even though he was married. My birth mother was forced to keep the family together, working many jobs to provide food and sometimes shelter when she could afford it.

My siblings didn't have much of a childhood. They took care of each other, and as soon as they could, they each left school for work to help with supporting the family. It was a hard life, far from what I experienced.

There were times my birth father would come home drunk, and my birth mom would make him breakfast–only to have him toss everything off the table onto the floor. One time he even knocked over a candle in the process, which started a fire in the home. One of my siblings quickly put it out.

As far as I can tell he attended only one wedding of his children, Allen's. He actually called to ask if he could still come to the wedding after getting out of jail, from a bar fight the night before.

The stories of him are not good ones. The only sibling that had a relationship with him was Grover. I guess being the first-born, they were able to forge some sort of bond. My sister, Delores, being the last child born before me, told me she only met him five our six times in her life. I'm certain I didn't miss much not knowing him. That said, I still owe him my life, even if I was conceived on a night he forced himself on my mother in a drunken state. At the time, even though he was not living with my mother, they were still married. They divorced in 1961, and he remarried. My father died in 1968 at the age of 54 from a heart attack.

Elizabeth, on the other hand, by all accounts was a strong, kind woman, who tried by all means to keep her family together. She worked multiple jobs, traying eggs and cleaning houses.

She cared deeply about her children and grandchildren. There were seven grandchildren when I was born, and 36 altogether, now 39, including my children. Even though she didn't have much at all, she always got something for each and everyone at Christmas.

Yes, my birth mother and the children were brought up Baptist, far from the Jewish background I grew up with. I have yet to figure out how she switched from growing up a Quaker to being Baptist. I suspect because it was my birthfather's religion.

From pictures I've seen of my mom, she was always around the grandchildren, and those that I've spoken with have fond memories of her. They all called her Gram. She passed away in 1992 at the age of 78.

Orville and Elizabeth circa 1931

Elizabeth with grandchild

Aunt Florence (Mom's sister) and Elizabeth

Elizabeth

Orville

Orville circa 1960's

Front Row: Amos, Delores, and Janice. Back Row: Leroy, Grover, Mom (Elizabeth), Ruth, Geneavie, and Orville (Charlie) in mid 1950's

Front Row: Grover, Leroy, and Allen. Back Row: Delores, Janice, and Amos in the early 1990's

The First Meeting ~ February 2013

It took about a month for me to arrange to get to Philadelphia/New Jersey to meet my siblings for the first time. During that month, I exchanged pictures with Ruth's daughters, Eva and MaryAnna, and grew excited about our first meeting.

It was Friday, February 22, 2013, when we flew into Philadelphia, stopped at my cousin Barbara's house, and then headed up to Ruth's house. Barbara had asked me if I was nervous, and I said, "No, not really." Ruth and I had spoken several times, and I felt like I knew her and her daughters.

Ruth and her husband, Walter, live in a house that Walter's parents built in the late 1800's. Walter was born in that house 85 years before our meeting. It's built on a 15-acre site in rural Stockton, New Jersey. As we drove to the house, deer crossed our path, and we had to stop and wait for them to cross the road.

As we entered the house, we had to duck to get in (people were shorter in the 1800's), and Eva, Ruth's daughter, greeted us. Moving to the family room, which was originally the dining room, we met Ruth and Walter for the first time. Ruth and I hugged, and she said, "I always hoped I would meet you one day," and she thanked the Lord for bringing us together.

For the next few hours we sat and talked about the circumstances of my adoption, what a good, strong woman our mother was, and what a bad guy our father was. We talked about the other siblings, both alive and deceased, and exchanged pictures of times past and present.

Ruth also told me stories of how my mother used to work multiple jobs, sometimes hitchhiking to get to work. Ruth also told me about the time she had picked up Mom to take her home. Ruth was on her bicycle with Mom riding on the handlebars. While on the way, she hit a rock, and Mom ended up breaking her arm in the fall.

The afternoon quickly turned into dinnertime, so we all went out to an Italian Restaurant in New Hope where we met Ruth's other daughter, MaryAnna, and Eva's husband, Jim and son James. After dinner we parted for the day, but we'd be back the next day to meet the other surviving siblings.

The next day, Joy and I would meet the other siblings at a gathering at MaryAnna's house. We stopped at Buckingham's Friends Cemetery, a Quaker cemetery, to pay my respects to my mother, Elizabeth Carver Snyder. She was buried in a Quaker cemetery with her parents, Robert Carver and Louise Doan and my brother, Kenneth, who died as an infant. Even though she was Baptist, her parents were Quakers, so she was allowed to be buried there.

Finding the cemetery was no easy feat, as it's entrance is between the Buckingham Friends Meeting House, an historic landmark founded in 1702 with the current building constructed in 1768, and a tool/utility vehicle storage building for the adjacent school.

In the Jewish religion, you leave a rock on the top of the tombstone to signify your visit. I brought a rock from my home in Florida to leave on her stone to signify my visit. Each time I have returned to the area, I've visited her, leaving a rock. I once was even there on her birthday.

We then proceeded to Maryanna's house in Milford, New Jersey, to meet the rest of the siblings. NOW I was nervous. I had not spoken to any of them, and unlike meeting with Ruth, I really didn't know what to expect.

Joy and I arrived there first. We saw a couple waiting in a car and assumed correctly that it was a sibling, who was waiting for another sibling, before coming in.

Ruth told us about each of the remaining siblings, so we sort of knew a little bit about each of them. She said, "Leroy is quiet, Amos speaks his mind with no filter, and Delores might be a little preoccupied with recent happenings with her great-grandson." All predictions were true.

Amos and Leroy, their wives Pat and Nancy, all walked in together along with Delores. Amos walked over to me and immediately said, "I expected to tell you that you looked like the milkman, but I have to say you look like a cross between brothers Grover and Allen." I think that was his way of acceptance.

Leroy was quiet, but I think that is part of his personality. I sat down close to him, and we spoke for a while, but I knew I'd have to meet with him alone to really talk to him. This is something I would do on our next visit.

Delores did seem a little preoccupied, but we did speak for a bit. When we took a family picture, the picture revealed how much of a resemblance there is between her and me.

They were all very accepting and welcoming. It was a wonderful day. I didn't want to leave, but I had promised my cousin, Barbara, that Joy and I would join her family for dinner. We were 30 minutes late, so we bid farewell to my siblings and thanked MaryAnna for hosting the reunion and I promised to be back soon–a promise we've kept many times since that first meeting.

Me reading the letter from the State of Florida to my siblings

Me reading the letter from the State of Florida to my siblings

First meeting picture of all surviving siblings. Front row: Delores and Ruth. Back Row: Me, Leroy, and Amos

First meeting picture: Ruth and Me

First meeting picture: Ruth's husband Walter and Leroy

First meeting picture: Amos and Me

Individual Sessions with Living Siblings

I went back three more times in 2013. In April and September with Joy, and in November I took my daughter, Melissa, to meet the new family.

April brought another visit to my mother's gravesite, but this time it was her birthday when we visited. It also brought individual visits with the remaining siblings.

We met Ruth at her house and visited for a few hours again sharing pictures and stories. My mother liked to crochet, and Ruth gave me a baby blanket that my mother had crocheted, probably for one of her great grandchildren, but none-the-less, I now had something my mother had made, so it was special.

This trip we were able to meet with Cathy and Robert, who are a niece and nephew from my sister, Genevieve. Genevieve passed away too young at, age 43, of cancer.

Duplex where my mother lived.
Pictured: Robert, Cathy, Me

We met in Frenchtown, New Jersey, where Cathy lived. While we had met Cathy on a previous visit, Robert drove in from his home in New York just to meet me. It was a fun meeting and Cathy pointed out two buildings that had some historic significance for me. First was a row house across the street from her house where my mother lived shortly after I was born. The second was a building on the main street of the town, where my mother's doctor's office was and where my mother lived in a rented apartment above the office before she passed away—sort of the start and finish for me, all in the same small town.

Later that day, we hooked up with my brother, Amos, and his wife, Pat, at their home. It's a beautiful piece of property with a pond stocked with fish and park benches around it to sit and enjoy the peaceful surroundings. Amos gave me many family pictures, and we sat out on his front porch and talked while enjoying the scenery.

That evening we visited my brother, Leroy, and his wife, Nancy. This proved to be a significant meeting, given the information Leroy shared with me that night.

We drove about 15 minutes from Milford to Frenchtown to get some pizza. During that dinner, Joy asked Leroy whether he knew about me.

Leroy then proceeded to tell us that not only did he know, but at 16 years old, he had heard Ruth and my mother arguing about the adoption. He then said he had wished all these years that he could have done something to help his mother, so that she could keep me. But honestly, what could he do, he was only 16 years old then. Leroy also told me he actually drove my mom to the hospital in Philadelphia to give birth to me. Then with tears in his eyes, he said "I've felt guilty all these years, and I'm so glad that you've had a good life." It was like a weight had been lifted off his shoulders.

Later that evening, I received more special gifts. Leroy gave me a pen and pencil set with wood insets that he made himself. Nancy showed us a serving plate made from post-depression glass, which she had kept for 30 years. She then gave it to me saying, "It was your mother's, and she would have wanted you to have it." Their generosity was unbelievable.

Since these first individual meetings, I've been back five times. I've had the opportunity to meet my brother Allen's daughters, Vicki and Tracy, and some of their families. I've met Amos' children and their families, and on a recent trip I've met my brother Orville's (Charlie) son Mike and his wife, Julie, from Texas. Charlie was the only sibling to move from the area; he lived in Kentucky.

I've also met some of Leroy's children, Wendy, David, and Nancy, and I look forward to meeting them all.

My daughter, Melissa, joined me on one trip and hit it off with my sister, Delores. We also found my father's grave in Lambertville, and again in the Jewish tradition, I left a rock from my home in Florida. He was buried with his second wife. No surprise there.

On another trip, I was able to find my paternal grandparents and great grandparents at yet another cemetery in the area.

Jeff and I went up last year, and he was able to meet all the remaining siblings. I think like me, he hit it off really well with Amos, as we sat and talked on his front porch for hours.

Each time I go back, I learn more and more, and become closer and closer to the family I never knew.

Surviving Siblings

Initially, I thought of writing about how my siblings grew up, getting stories from each remaining member of the Snyder clan. However, what became very apparent to me, first through the letter I received from the State of Florida, and later in discussions with my siblings, is that they had a very hard life growing up.

They moved from relative to relative for a roof over their heads. Many times there was not enough to eat, and our father was in and out of their lives. One sibling was even given to my paternal grandparents to raise. My father forced my mother to leave him at their farm. In my first meeting with Leroy, I commented on what big hands our father had, and his response was that they were even bigger as they were coming at your face.

Based on all this, I had to change how I was going to write this chapter. The siblings would rather forget about this painful time, and I understand. While I had my trials and tribulations growing up, it was certainly nowhere near what they had to endure. In this chapter I'm going to give you my first impressions of the remaining siblings and I've also asked their children to talk about what they remember growing up, and thoughts about my mother, who they referred to as Gram.

Ruth

My mother, Elizabeth; Ruth's husband, Walter; and Ruth

Ruth was born in 1933 and has five children. Leaving school at 13 years old to begin to help support the family, she worked her way up in a local supermarket chain to Deli Manager.

From everything I've seen, she is a no-nonsense, take-charge person, from her family life to her work life. On the flip side, she has been so kind and accepting of me. She is also a deeply religious person.

I do wish that I had met her earlier in life as today she has some health problems that limit her interaction.

I had asked the siblings a series of questions to attempt to understand their thoughts of growing up. Here are Ruth's responses to those questions:

What are your most vivid memories of growing up?
> *I took care of my brothers and sisters, so that our mom could work to feed us.*

What are the most vivid memories from your adult life?
> *Working hard and raising my kids. I stayed at home until Eva was about two years old.*

What are the most vivid memories of your mother?
> *She worked hard to keep all the kids together so everyone would know each other. She was strict with us, but also loved us and took care of us. She would hitchhike to clean houses, but it really wasn't hitchhiking, as it was people*

who knew her and saw her walking, so they would stop and pick her up.

What are the most vivid memories of your father?
He was not home much, and he didn't really help mom. He was a drinker.

What do you enjoy most today?
When relatives come to visit.

Who was the biggest influence in your life? And why?
Mom. Taught me my work ethic.

If you had a do over for anything in your past what would it be and why?
Nothing–Walt and I have had a good life together. He's my soulmate.

What did you do to earn a living? Did you enjoy it?
I was a meat department/deli manager in a grocery store. Yes.

What is your favorite food?
I enjoy Italian food.

What did Mom make that you especially liked to eat?
Mom used to make us lima beans and spaghetti. We didn't have much back then.

What's your favorite vacation place? Why?
We did driving vacations to visit Charlie in Kentucky, and we visited one of our favorite places, Nashville.

Do you have any hobbies?
I used to make porcelain dolls. Don't do it much anymore.

If there was one thing you could pass on to your children what would it be?
I would tell them to have good communication with their spouse, discuss things, work on things. That makes for a happy, respectful marriage.

What are your thoughts on the reunion with me?
I'm so happy we met... I thought about you from time to time over the years and had hoped you had a good life.

To supplement my questions/interview is a submission from her daughter MaryAnna:

Thoughts and remembrances of my mom....Ruth. Being the eldest daughter, Ruth left school before finishing 8th grade. She stayed at home to care for her younger siblings, enabling her mother to go to work, and she worked to help make ends meet. She had to grow up fast, a happy childhood eluded her. The family moved around a lot.

Mom was a stay-at-home mom for a good number of years. When Eva turned 2 years old, Mom returned to Acme Markets in Flemington, NJ. Mom continued to work for Acme in the Meat Dept. and as Deli Manager up until her retirement. One thing that would always amazed me was when Mom would do her weekly inventory and orders for the following week, her ability to add a column of numbers in her head. Mom was exceptional in math.

Mom & Dad always made sure we went to Sunday school each week, plus attended Youth Choir and B.Y.F groups. I remember when Mom was baptized and became more involved at Baptistown

Baptist Church. For many years she co-directed the Junior B.Y.F group. She was very hands on and would always do the activities with the kids. Growing up in our house a personal faith in God was very important–and still is.

Mom always wanted us to do things that she never had the opportunity to do. We attended Montrose Bible Camp in the summers. We all had some type of music lessons through the years. Steve had voice, Le had guitar, MaryAnna had piano, voice and accordion, Walt had banjo, and Eva piano. Mom even took lessons on the dobro for a short time. Activities also included 4-H clubs, girl scouts, cub scouts, Indian guides, to name a few. Mom made sure we kept cool in the summer with an above ground pool in our yard. Roller Skating was a favorite past time for all of us. It was always fun when we would go skating, and our cousins would be there too.

We would always visit our cousins, or they would come to our house. Each trip in our car would have us all singing songs together. One of my favorite childhood memories.

Our family Thanksgiving gatherings were always epic. Cousins, aunts and uncles and massive amounts of food. We would exchange names with cousins for Christmas gifts, and the aunts and uncles would do couple exchanges. Memorial Day would find us at Aunt Janice's in Frenchtown where we would watch the parade from her house.

For years Mom and Dad would play pinochle every Saturday night with Uncle Orville and Aunt Barbara. Sherry and I would go roller skating, and they always took a break when it was time to pick us up. In the summer, Uncle Orville would take us out on his boat/pontoon for a day of swimming or water skiing on the Delaware River. This continued up to the time Uncle Orville moved his family to Murray, KY. Uncle Orville would always tease his sister. He loved to play pranks.

Mom's hobby has been ceramics. She took many classes on techniques always working to be better. She began making porcelain dolls and she was so talented! The girls in our family each have a beloved doll or two that Mom made. She was very talented in this department.

I think Mom's heart's desire was to give her children a better life than she had growing up. I believe she did the best she could with what she had. I really wouldn't change anything from our childhood. (Except I would have gotten a washer and dryer sooner than we did...least favorite thing–going to laundromats.)

Mom would never speak of her father. She also would not tolerate alcohol in our house. This was because of her father's drinking. I didn't know my mom's father. I only saw him twice. But, I remember when Mom got the call telling of his death....she cried.

My memories of Gram are filled with love and emotion. She was frail in body, but strong in spirit. She knew how to love big with every fiber of her being. Her love for family is the legacy she has given each of us.

I remember as a young girl picking berries along the road and bringing them back to the house to make a cake together. I loved visiting with her and sharing that special time together–just the two of us. I remember the many meals she would make–especially roast beef and always with gravy. She would always end her meal with a slice of bread on her plate, then she'd pour on lots of gravy–it was her 'dessert'. For the holidays, Gram always made her "Raisin Cake" and "Rice Pudding"...both big family favorites.

We would talk for hours sharing all that what was going on in my life. Then she would share all the details of all the other grandchildren–good, bad, happy or sad. Gram was a worrier. I think she thrived on the drama that would be going on in one of her children's or grandchildren's lives–because she was the type that always needed to be needed. And we all needed her in many different ways. We loved her depth of caring–which was immeasurable. She loved to crochet–she made baby blankets, sweater sets and many other items. With each new arrival Gram would be sure the baby had at least one of her creations. Even the grandchildren, who had not yet had children, she made sure she completed a set for them too...for the children yet to come.

One specific time that I drove Gram home to her apartment in Frenchtown, NJ (over Dr. King's office), we sat in my car talking about family, my mom and when she was younger. At one point Gram began to cry. While trying to comfort her, she said to me, "I never got to hold him. They wouldn't let me hold him." At this time I thought she was speaking of her son Kenneth, who had died at a very young age. So I tried to make her feel better, and then I changed the subject.

But now we all know about her sacrifice of giving Sol up for adoption and the emotional struggle she lived with–I believe on that day she was speaking of the day she brought Sol into the world and never had the chance to welcome him or whisper in his ear how much she loved him and tell him how hard it was to let him go.

Gram's strength and faith saw her through a life of hardships, joys and love. I think of her often, and I am forever grateful for all she has given us. We all love and miss her every day.

Me, James, Eva, Zach, Walter, MaryAnna, Melissa, Le

Ruth, Walter, and Jeff

Amos, Ruth, and Leroy

Ruth and Walter

Leroy

Nancy and Leroy

Leroy was born in 1939. He and Nancy raised four children. Leroy, who is sometimes called Roy, is a quiet, easy going gentleman. He was a steel fabricator and later a draftsman, and worked many years for the same company.

Leroy is very proud of his home, and to this day, he still insists on cutting his own lawn. He is very meticulous, which I saw in his pens and pencils that he carves. Leroy also loves animals, and we got to meet Trixie, his pug. In spite of her health issues, Trixie was part of the family, and Leroy loved her immensely. I have very much enjoyed our chats.

Leroy also answered a series of questions for me to get to know him and his life growing up:

What are your most vivid memories of growing up?
All of the kids taking care of each other. Also that I used to fly planes as a teen. I soloed at 16 in an L6, which was an open-air cockpit plane used for training. It was a distraction as we hung out at the airfield rather than on the streets.

What are the most vivid memories from your adult life?
Working hard and raising my kids.

What are the most vivid memories of your mother?
She tried very hard and did the best she could for her family. It was not easy, she had a hard life.

What are the most vivid memories of your father?

I remember a train ride we took once from Lambertville to Frenchtown. Also I remember him sometimes driving a truck. When I turned 17, he had me drive him around and take him to bars, even though I hated his drinking.

What do you enjoy most today?
Seeing the kids and grandkids.

Who was the biggest influence in your life? And why?
I went to work at 13 in a restaurant in Flemington. The two owners, both Jewish, took me under their wing. I remember failing English once, and one of the owners insisted I go back to school in Elizabeth to pass the class. A lot of strangers helped me out along the way.

If you had a do-over for anything in your past what would it be and why?
I would have got a lot more education.

What did you do to earn a living? Did you enjoy it?
I was a steel fabricator, and I also was a machine designer and draftsman. I designed a couple of machines that saved the company I worked for a lot of hours. They said what I was suggesting wouldn't work, but I came in over a weekend and built my design and proved it would work. I loved a challenge.

What is your favorite food?
Meat and potatoes.

What did Mom make that you especially liked to eat?
Fried potatoes.

What's your favorite vacation place? Why?
We did driving vacations to Nashville, Florida, and a bunch of other places.

Do you have any hobbies?
I used to make pens. Now my granddaughter can do it.

If there was one thing you could pass on to your children what would it be?
Be nice to people. Don't intentionally insult or hurt anyone.

What are your thoughts on the reunion with me?
I'm happy your life turned out well. It's really a burden off me, as I still think I should have done something back when you were born.

Below is a submission by Leroy's daughter, Wendy, on thoughts on her father and Gram:

As I am sure you have come to understand, my father is a pretty private person, and I have certainly inherited that characteristic from him, so I have struggled a bit with your request. Despite that, I think it would be a shame if your book did not include a little something about my father and his triumphs–made even more notable considering his difficult childhood. So, here goes....

There was never a doubt that my father loved us more than anything and that he would do anything for his kids. Some of my earliest memories are of my father tucking my sister and me into bed, saying our prayers, and getting a kiss. This happened every night in the bedroom Nancy and I shared in the addition my father put on our first house on Railroad Avenue. I remember him building that addition, with some help from neighbors and uncles, almost literally with his own two hands. That was before we moved to the new house on Dawn Rd, which in 1972 was considered to be a very prestigious address. We were all so proud to move into the brand new house.

My father always worked hard, sometimes two jobs at a time. He instilled in all of us a very strong work ethic and sense of responsibility. Although Dad worked hard, he did find time to have fun with us. I remember Sundays at the roller rink with Uncle Al and Aunt Gen and their kids. Dad indulged the humiliation of donning a feather, headband, and leather vest when I wanted to join the Indian Princesses. He coached little league baseball for several years while David and Roy played. He never missed their games when they played pee wee, midget and high school football. We went on several family vacations–always long drives somewhere–Florida, Tennessee, Virginia–and took yearly day trips to the shore–Point Pleasant or Seaside Heights.

My dad has a great singing voice and can yodel. I fondly remember riding in the car with him while he sang every song on the radio, "A white sport coat and a pink carnation..." And he taught himself to play the guitar and piano. I understand he sang to their dog Trixie all the time and comforted her on her last night with them by sitting with her most of the night, much of the time singing to her.

Dad can fix anything and can figure out any math problem–it's a shame he didn't have a chance to go to college, he would probably have been an engineer. Dad did all of the work on the family cars and lawn mowers, and he made a couple of go-carts for the boys. He took a lot of pride in keeping his lawn mowed, and I'm sure it bothers him now that he's having a harder time keeping up with that big yard. My husband has frequently called Dad for advice on fixing something around the house, and Dad is never stumped.

In short, I am humbled when I think about the sharp contrast between Dad's father and the kind of father Dad is/was to the four of us.

A few things about Gram:

She ate a lot of toast with peanut butter. She made the best rice pudding and raisin cake on earth.

She was always for the underdog. It seemed the more trouble one of her grandchildren got into, the more she supported them.

She remembered each and every grandchild and their spouses at Christmas–whether it was a pair of socks, a piece of jewelry from the 5 and 10 cent store, or in one case–a stick of deodorant.

She was independent and tough when it came to dealing with the adversities that always seem to find her.

I saw her a week or so before she died, and she told me she was at peace and was ready to go. That visit has always given me comfort and hope that I will depart this earth with the same dignity.

Below is a submission from Leroy's daughter, Nancy, on thoughts of her father and Gram:

Wendy sent me a copy of what she said about Dad. She expressed many of the same things I remember. I just wanted to add a few things.

I, too, remember Dad singing. I don't remember the name of the song, but some of the words were "put your head on my shoulder."

We went camping sometimes with Uncle Grover and Uncle Al.

Every weekend was spent with family at someone's house, at the roller rink, or camping.

As the oldest, I grew up in the house on Railroad Ave. I loved it there and was not very happy with the move. Dad was so proud and happy, I got over it.

I was Dad's scorekeeper when he coached little league and when we went bowling.

When the first Monday night football game aired, he let me stay up to watch it with him.

He and my husband took a damaged [Chevy] Vega, fixed it, and that was my first car.

He always seemed happy when we were growing up. I could go on and on, but I think you get the picture.

A couple of things about Gram:

I was the first granddaughter, so I may have gotten some special attention.

I never heard her raise her voice, and now when my husband can't hear me, he calls it my 'Betty voice' and this is meant as a compliment. He loved her as much as I did.

When I was older, I would take her grocery shopping and loved just being with her. I miss her still.

Leroy and Nancy

Me, Wendy, Melissa, Nancy, Grace (Grover's Wife), and Leroy

Leroy and Me

Jeff, Nancy and Leroy

Amos

Pat and Amos

Amos was born in 1940 and is a real no-nonsense kind of guy. From the first time we met, he said whatever was on his mind. He is as they say "salt of the earth," good guy. No pretense, no bullshit. At first, he puts forth this tough exterior, but he is truly about family first; he'd do anything for his kids and his wife, Pat.

He talks about Pat as his "old lady," his "ball and chain," but you can see he loves her so much. Together they have raised a wonderful family, all much like them, they are hard working, straight shooters.

Amos likes to tinker with cars, trucks and other mechanical equipment. He's also kept animals from a donkey and horses, to dogs and cats.

Amos and I have forged a pretty good relationship over the past three years. I so enjoying talking with him, and we talk fairly regularly, either he calls me or I call him.

Amos also answered a series of questions for me to get to know him and his life growing up:

What are your most vivid memories of growing up?
The first 20 years of my life, I put it behind me. I'm glad this all came about, but it brought back old memories I would rather not relive.

What are the most vivid memories from your adult life?
> *Going into the Army, getting married, having kids, grandkids. Pat and I raised four great kids.*

What are the most vivid memories of your mother?
> *She was a great lady. She gave us all that she could.*

What are the most vivid memories of your father?
> *Didn't really know him.*

What do you enjoy most today?
> *The kids, the grandkids, and sitting on my porch.*

Who was the biggest influence in your life? And why?
> *Our father, I saw him as being something I never wanted to be. Unlike him, I was always there for my kids as I still am today. Going in the Army helped me.*

If you had a do over for anything in your past what would it be and why?
> *Some of the financial decisions I made.*

What did you do to earn a living? Did you enjoy it?
> *Drive trucks and heavy equipment. Yes.*

What is your favorite food?
> *Meat and potatoes and homemade soup.*

What did mom make that you especially liked to eat?
> *Raisin Cake and rice pudding. My oldest daughter has Gram's recipes and makes me Raisin Cake every Thanksgiving.*

What's your favorite vacation place? Why?
Always worked through them, because I usually had off winter months, and we would go to see in-laws in Georgia.

Do you have any hobbies?
I used to like to have animals to take care of. Too old now.

If there was one thing you could pass on to your children what would it be?
There's no "me" in marriage. Kids come first. Be good parents, give your kids time, make them listen and be respectful. When they're out of the house, do what you can to help them, do not support them; they have to find their own way.

What are your thoughts on the reunion with me?
I thought it was great. I hope it continues. Anytime you need to talk, call me. I'll be the big brother with the common sense. Have to meet your kids.

Below is a submission by Amos' daughter, Sandy, on thoughts on her father and Gram:

My Dad

What to say about my Dad? There is so much I can say. Dad is as real as it gets. Some people may not like what he says, but he says it like he sees it. He's a straight shooter. Pride, honest, and integrity, are all words I could use to describe my Dad. He is tough as nails, but at the same time he is compassionate, and would do anything he could to help someone. He is not a judging person, he takes people as they come to him. Dad doesn't like to be around phony people. He always says, "The only person I am better than is the son of a bitch who thinks he's better than me."

He loves to tease people, but he only does because he loves you. He has a lot of what I like to call Dadisms. He says things like, "Quit the grab ass," which actually means quit messing around before someone gets hurt. Heard that one a lot growing up. Here are a few more, "You're poking a bear with a stick" (don't make your mother mad), "Nothing but shit comes out of an asshole," "Cat got an ass, bird got feathers."

Dad has worked hard his whole life to give to his family. His family is everything to him. Dad and Mom both sacrificed so that we could have what we needed. Dad always tells me that there are no perfect men left like him, and that Mom is lucky she got the last one. Little does he know, I really do think that he is the best man on the planet. My mom may have been lucky, but we were lucky to have him too!

Things I remember about Gram:

She never forgot anyone's birthday or anyone at Christmas. Trust me, there were a lot to remember. Gram always made sure she had something for everyone. When I was little, she would make me a nightgown. As I grew, sometimes it was money in a card. She didn't have a lot of money, but somehow she did it.

Gram made everyone of her grandchildren a sweater set for their first-born child. She would even ask what color you wanted it to be. You had your choice of white, yellow, green, blue or pink. She gave me mine when I was 16 years old. I chose yellow. She wanted to make sure all of us had one before she passed away. When I had my son at age 31, I used the sweater set to bring him home. Of course, I still have it and will never part with it.

Dad would go pick Gram up on Sundays a lot to spend the day with us. She always brought rice pudding and raisin cake. Her rice pudding was the best! Dad always loved her raisin cake.

The bottom line is I saw Gram as sweet, but also as a very strong woman that loved her family very much. She raised all of her children by herself. Since I am a single mom with only one child, I can't imagine how hard that must have been.

Amos

Amos

Amos, Jeff, Derek, Amy, Pat, Sandy, and Delores

Delores

Lester and Delores

Delores was born in 1945 and is the closest sibling in age to me, born 12 years before. She has raised kids, grandkids, and even great grandkids. Time and time again she takes relatives in, due to her caring and good nature. She is a hard worker, and even today she continues to work to provide for herself and other family members when they reach out to her.

We talk from time to time, and I do enjoy our conversations as they are free flowing and about everything under the sun. She truly cares more about others than she does for herself. I believe her work ethic and caring absolutely come from our mother.

Delores also answered a series of questions for me to get to know her and her life growing up:

What was your most vivid memory growing up?
Watching American Bandstand with my sister, Janice, at the age of 10. Being more of an adult than a child. We all had to grow up fast.

What was your most vivid memories from your adult life?
Work and survival. Thanksgiving and Christmas when we all got together.

What are your most vivid memories of your mother?
Hard worker, kind.

What are your most vivid memories of your father?
Didn't know him, saw him about four times in my life, and

he was "under the weather" those times.

What do you enjoy most today?
Talking with my daughters: Lisa, Donna, Janette. Spending time with my niece, Jean, my sister Janice's oldest daughter. Spending time with my great grandson, Nick. Sitting on Amos' porch and going to the casino occasionally.

Who was the biggest influence on your life? And why?
My mom. She taught me about work ethic, the only way to survive.

If you had to do over anything in your past what would it be and why?
I would not have gotten married so young, because I was not able to give my children the attention they deserved.

What did you do to earn a living? Did you enjoy it?
Many jobs. Yes, because every one I did, I took away a new knowledge and accomplishment.

What is your favorite food?
Meat and potatoes (snack chips), Italian

What did Mom make that you especially liked to eat?
Homemade cinnamon rolls, donuts.

What's your favorite vacation place? Why?
Colorado is beautiful, and so is Massachusetts where my daughters live. But I also enjoy a couple of days in Atlantic City from time to time because there are so many memories there with my children, grandchildren, nieces, nephews, sister, and friends, over the years.

Do you have any hobbies?
No, but I do enjoy reading.

If there was one thing you could pass on to your children what would it be?
They all work very hard, so I would like them to enjoy the little things in life, slow down, and be happy.

What are your thoughts on the reunion with me?
I think it's great to have a younger brother, and I hope to get to know you better. I'm just a phone call away.

Below is a submission from Dee's daughter, Lisa, about her mother and Gram:

4/19/15

Today would have been Gram's birthday. I jotted down just a few things about growing up and about Mom, but to be honest I really don't know much that's personal about Mom.

Mom was 14 when she became pregnant with my brother Rick. She had me, Donna, Janette and Leslie by the time she was 22 years old (or somewhere-thereabouts). She never finished grammar school due to the pregnancy, but later on she took and passed her GED. I was a young teen when she did that, and I was very proud of her.

When we were all very little, we lived in Milford on Water Street in Aunt Gen's pink house. I remember a big Thanksgiving get together in the basement. I think my dad and Uncle Roy worked at a welding company, at about this time, and my dad lost his hearing and had to wear hearing aids. He was labeled as disabled, and so jobs that he could land were on horse farms and such.

We moved out to a farm. Mom and Dad were the caretakers to a large horse farm, and we lived in a farmhouse with our ponies, horses, chickens, mini-bikes, go-carts, etc. Gram lived with us then. I remember making applesauce from the apple trees and gathering around the kitchen table with the butcher to cut venison that my dad and Rick got. Aunts and uncles and cousins would come out to the farm. Mom raised, bred, and sold Lhasa Apsos. Mom cleaned homes and offices during the day and worked the graveyard shift at Bemus Bags, all at the same time.

She came to our school events, when she could, and supported each of us when we took on a sport or instrument.

I remember going to drive-in movies and going to Great Adventure park. All of us kids, and a friend for each, of course, loaded into the station wagon. What chaos! With us kids there was always more kids hanging around, and Mom always welcomed all. Rick had several, "no-where-to-live" friends living up in the attic for some time. There were always extra people living with us over the years. The more the merrier, I guess, but honestly Mom would not turn anyone away that needed a place to stay.

Years later, Gram, Mom and I cleaned a hotel in Frenchtown on Saturdays. We always had lunch afterwards. That was one of the things I remember–years earlier, Mom sometimes needed an extra hand to help clean her houses, and she would let me help. It took me away from school sometimes, but we always went out to lunch when we cleaned. That was my reward, but really I was so happy to go out to lunch, just a simple little deli, but I always felt so special just to be out with her. I don't remember much alone time with Mom. She was always working.

We moved a few more times. My father really wasn't much help in supporting her or the family. Mom did it all. Dad had some problems, but Mom was a rock.

What more can I say about Mom?–She'd give you her last dime, and has many times to so many people. Many that took advantage of her. She cares with all her heart, which sometimes gets her heart stepped on. She works hard and rarely spends money on herself. She enjoys a rare trip to the casinos, her only escape from her life. She lives on less and asks for even less from others.

I feel like Mom has gotten a bum rap from life. From such an early age becoming a mother, a child herself, working and busting her butt to provide what she could with the little money she had. She deserves a better life. She worked long and hard, and it's time that life gives her a break. I'm hoping that I can be part of the break.

Melissa and Delores - 2013

Siblings That Have Passed

For those siblings that have passed away, I've asked a niece or nephew to tell me about my siblings, so that I might get to know a little about the person they were.

Grover

Grover

Grover was the oldest and was 23 years old and married with children when I was born. I have been to meet his wife, Grace, and have seen their family home. Grover liked to collect clocks, which was apparent by the hundreds of all types in their home.

Unfortunately, I have not been able to contact any of his children at this point in time, so all I can do is recount excerpts of his obituary to convey who Grover was.

He was married for 53 years when he passed away in 2003. Born in 1932, he had four sons, and he lived in Milford, New Jersey.

Grover was a service manager at a Pontiac dealership for 37 years. He was a crossing guard for the Milford School District and was a member of the Milford Volunteer Fire Company and the Milford Rescue Squad.

Update: I have recently had a conversation with his son Walter and plan to meet him in the not too distant future.

Grover, Grace, Grover Jr., Barry, and Walt

Grace and Grover

Walter, Grace, Grover, Barry, and Kevin

Orville (Charlie)

Orville Charles
graduation -1953

Much of what I've come to know about my brother Orville is from stories told by the remaining siblings and from a personal meeting and several conversations with his son, Mike, and his daughter, Sherry. Orville's wife and daughters live in Kentucky, and I hope to meet them some day.

My brother, Orville, was born in 1934. He was nicknamed Charlie. Charlie, like the others, had it tough growing up. He didn't move around as much as the rest of the family. He had a roof over his head and food on the table thanks to our paternal grandparents. This was because one of the times when the family had no place to live, my paternal grandparents took them in. As told by my sister, Ruth, my paternal grandmother took a liking to Charlie, who was a baby at the time. When it came time to move out of their home, my father ordered my mother to leave Charlie behind to be raised by my paternal grandparents.

There was nothing my mother could do but leave him. Charlie didn't know this and held the belief for many years that my mother didn't love him. At some point, he confided in Ruth, who told him of the circumstances of why he was left with his grandparents.

Charlie and his wife, Barbara, had four children. He drove a truck for a bakery and was a janitor at a school. He loved baseball and he coached his son, Mike, in little league. He also umpired baseball games.

Charlie had a passion for raising and showing Bull Terriers. In 1972, he had the top female Bull Terrier in the country named

Charlie with his dog, Lady Jane, Best of Breed

Lady Jane. He and his wife, Barbara, owned a Bull Terrier kennel named Paradise Kennels. A picture of Charlie and Lady Jane can be seen in a book, *Your Bull Terrier* by Marilyn Drewes, published in 1978.

Owning the kennel and breeding dogs was not easy. When he first started he needed the help of a judge from New York to get the official papers for one of the dogs he was breeding. He knew the judge from some side work he would do, one of those jobs was cutting the judge's lawn.

Several of Charlie's prized dogs were stolen, and he was heartbroken about it. About a week after the incident, Charlie had a heart attack, and he passed away several days later.

I was told an interesting adoption story about Charlie's son, Mike, who is my nephew. As a teenager, Mike had relations with a girl, and she became pregnant. The girl gave birth to a son. Unfortunately the girl died during childbirth, and the child was put up for adoption.

Julie, Jeff, Me, and Mike

Recently, that child found Mike, and they have connected and have a good relationship. His son lives in the Philadelphia area and has a wife and children of his own, one of which he named after his mother, whom he never knew.

Below is a submission from Charlie's daughter, Sherry, about her father:

Things I remember about my Dad, Orville Charles (Charlie) Snyder

At the time I was born we lived in Milford, New Jersey. At about two years old, we moved to Upper Black Eddy, Pennsylvania. Dad would say taxes were not as high in Pennsylvania. We lived there until I was 15 (1960-1973).

My dad told me until us kids came along he could make a living betting the horses, or he said he would bet on the Jockey. When I started school, my father was the janitor at Bridgeton Elementary. I remember getting in trouble in first grade and having to stand in the hallway and my dad was cleaning that hall. It was still good having him there though. He took a very active role in our raising. He loved to play with us. We had a big field beside our house and the neighbors would come over, and we would all play baseball or softball. Dad coached my girls softball team, and when not coaching he would umpire boys and girls games. He was good at it. All my friends enjoyed him. He taught me well, and today, I still continued to played softball on coed leagues here in Kentucky.

We always had a boat in our backyard on the Delaware River. At age eight, dad taught me how to water ski. We would all go swimming out in the middle of the river on our pontoon boat. He put ropes on the sides of it so we could hang on as we floated down river. We also hung on so we could hide and play river tag. I spent my summers playing softball, swimming, and fishing. Dad taught me how to drive the boat, and by age ten I was allowed to take my friends out in the boat by myself, and I could teach them to ski.

We would go to Regal Ridge Day Camp every summer. We would walk over the Milford Bridge and catch the bus at the firehouse in New Jersey. When we got home, we had newspaper routes and papers to deliver by bike (Mike and me at first and then Susan, when she was old enough). Dad also delivered newspapers by car. We enjoyed delivering papers, as we got to keep our money. It helped us pay for roller skating on the weekends with our cousins, and we were able to buy our own gifts for each other. MaryAnna would go skating with us while Aunt Ruth, Uncle Walt, Mom, and Dad played Pinnacle. I think the girls won a lot more than the guys. They would play until 2 am.

I guess we didn't have a lot of money because mom reminds me we ate a lot of soup and pasta, but I always felt rich.

Dad drove a semi-truck for a while, when I was in high school. I think he missed us because he always sent us postcards. If he were on the road for a long time, he'd buy us something and give it to us when he got home.

He built the dog kennel and we raised bull terriers, and I had a Bedlington terrier. We learned how to show them, and one year my puppy won best puppy in show at the Atlantic City boardwalk. Dad's bull terriers won often, and he became known for having some of the best quality dogs. He was always careful who he would sell them to. He wanted to make sure they were all in good caring hands.

We moved to Murray Kentucky in 1973 because the neighborhood was becoming overrun with illegal drugs. I was asked where I would like to move, and since we would always read about Kentucky in history books, Kentucky it was–but it had to be by water. We ended up in Murray, Kentucky.

Dad built a new kennel and mom groomed dogs after she was

trained in New York. I was able to go with her for training on the day they learned about Bedlington Terriers, since I had to learn to care for my own dog.

Dad umpired baseball and softball in Murray until he had a retinal detachment. He had some issues with double vision for a while, and afterwards, he never returned to umpiring. He became a runner. He and his five dogs would run three miles a day. He would always run a half or a full marathon on his birthday. He did it there at the house on a one-mile track we have, through the woods and down the lane. We entered short 5K's together as the years rolled on. On the Fourth of July, it got to be a family affair to run the Main Street Mile in Murray. The grandkids, kids, and other family members all participated.

Thanksgiving in Upper Black Eddy and in Murray, was always a big family get together. Thanksgiving was almost as great as Christmas.

Christmas holidays were always great. Dad went all out with lighting. All of us, including Mom, Dad, kids, and grandkids, would go on an outing to search for the perfect tree. We'd pile in his van and spend the day searching. We even took one of the dogs with us. Our search would take us to a piece of land between the lakes. We'd take cookies, hot chocolate, a chain saw, and a trailer to haul the tree.

Dad would watch my children after school, while I was still at work. He worked his schedule around so that he could play with them until I got there. They would play kick the can and basketball. Dad supported me going to college, so that I would be the first one in our family to go to college. He was proud of me, and I could always go to him to get answers.

Dad died from a heart attack. It happened when he was so devastated about some puppies that were stolen from the kennel. The puppies were recovered, but Dad was gone and didn't get to know that.

He was a good man who took pride in his work and loved his kennel and dogs. He loved his family, wife, kids, and grandkids.

Back Row: Barbara, Mike, Charlie. Front Row: Susan, Sharon, Sherry.

Main Street Mile - Murray, Kentucky in 1992. Back Row: Marsha, Charlie, Sherry, Richard, and Susan. Front Row: Sherry's sons: Ben and David and Susan's son: Terry.

Allen

Allen was born in 1936, and he passed away in 1991, at the age of 55. He raised three daughters.

Below is a submission from his daughters, Vicki and Tracy, about memories of their father and Gram:

I think Dad was most known by most of the nieces and nephews, and probably his siblings, as the clown of the group. He never really grew up. He was always the one either playing with or teasing everyone, and he loved a practical joke, for a reaction!

He played guitar and piano and yodeled. He could not read notes well. He would ask us kids to teach him notes when we took piano lessons, and he could get the right hand, but he then just gave up because he played piano terrifically by ear and the guitar. He always wished he could read notes, and I (Tracy) always wished I could play half as good as he. My youngest son (AJ) played guitar and reminded me of him sometimes because he would tend to just play what he heard more than concentrate on the notes. I loved sitting in the room with him when he played, and I still have his last guitar. It is not worth anything, just sentimental, remembering sitting with him while he played.

He would always play around the campfire when we camped with Aunt Gen and Uncle Grover. We were loud and stayed around the campfire until early morning hours. Vicki and I both truly wished we had a recording to remember the yodeling; he had a great voice and enjoyed showing it. We mean that in the funniest way because shy was not him!!

He and Mom loved to dance. Everyone always waited to watch them dance together. Their polka and jitterbug–we can still see in our mind–they moved as one! He had such agility, and Mom always had to keep up–never sure what show-off move would come next. Also, whenever there was a wedding (or any place with a microphone) he usually ended up yodeling. He did at both of our weddings.

He used to dress up at Halloween and go to different people's houses and not say a word. He would go in, and just sit on their couch or lie on their bed, and scare them because they did not know who he was. He would stay silent for the longest time, so that he could really scare them. He didn't give up. Even as a grandfather this continued–he went out trick or treating with Jen and always had to be in costume to march in the Frenchtown Parade with her. Oh what fun he had in life!

My cousin Cathy also shared with us at dinner that when she had medical issues and had to have surgery, how dad would go there the night before and make her laugh. He joked about getting her out of there, or comforting her fears by telling how to hide under the bed when the doctor or nurses came in. Oh how Aunt Gen would love to have "hung" him!!! I can still picture the look on her face!!! He loved a reaction!

I remember as a kid all of the kids came to our house to play "kick the can" because Dad always played with us.

Dad also bought and sold things constantly. He used to drive my husband Darryl crazy because he would need a tractor, and he worked in the industry and could find used ones at a decent price or get them at cost. He would help Dad get a good deal, and then Dad would use it for a season and then sell it, and need another! The cars he bought never worked. We camped with Aunt Gen and

Uncle Grover, and most Friday nights the camper would be all hooked up, and then the car wouldn't start, or something would be wrong.

Dad thrived on how young he always felt and was very proud to show someone up in such a fun way. He was an avid bike rider and thought nothing of jumping on his bike and taking a 20-mile bike ride–occasionally dragging us and the neighborhood kids along. There were never too many kids for him. He also loved how after that bike ride everyone would be winded except, of course, him. It was so frustrating because we were half his age, and he was never winded!!

Through our entire childhood and into our early teens, we took some neighborhood kids and met Aunt Gen and her family at the Roller Rink. He could skate as well as he danced, and again he loved to show it!!! Through grandparenting we continued the roller skating–he taught my youngest to skate and bought her, her first pair of skates at the age of 2–they weighed as much as she did. She was amazing–and still is on skates–both of the girls were fortunate enough to have those memories.

He also loved to fish, and thought he was great at that too, but in actuality he never really caught anything. When our oldest son, Doug, was 2, we lived by a river, and he would always come and take him fishing. Doug was very serious, so he would sit forever, as long as he started with a clean diaper. Dad was good to take him for a couple of hours, as long as he didn't have to deal with that.

How about our Thanksgivings as kids–just think of all those siblings, spouses and then us kids–OMG, just the thought brings back all the crowds, the laughs, the fun, and who was sitting at the kid table...

Sibling Rivalry–Dad and Aunt Ruth worked together at a local grocery store: she in the meat department, he in the produce department–she being the more serious of the two–he being the clown. The stories he came home with, the practical jokes he played, and how mad she would be, just made his day!!! He was a character! Mom always said when he left the store that was a great day for Aunt Ruth. Again this was always 'in fun'.

Dad would never have been an 'old person'–he loved a challenge –taking the kids to the park would mean he got to go on all the slides, swings, etc. When Dad turned 35, all of us kids teased him that he was half way to 70. He did not like that, he was definitely on the vain side. All in all he loved life and doing things, and the most important thing to him was his family and his grandchildren. Until he died, he was at every sport game that Jen or Doug played. The others were too young, but for Jen and Doug, he was always there, or at our houses playing with them, or taking them somewhere.

His Dad–I (Vicki) know their father was not exactly a stand up guy–but I will always remember Dad telling how his father called the night before his wedding to see if it was OK if he still came –as he had been in a "altercation" the night before hence "a bar room brawl" as he described it! Dad always said his wedding was the only wedding of any of the siblings his father attended. There was a certain amount of pride with that. My thoughts go to whatever he did, he was still his father, and cared. I only remember meeting him a few times; he was a big man, and a tease, and intimidating to me.

Gram was a very quiet and sincere type of person, with a lot of sadness and challenges through the years. Writing this makes me wonder–was Dad more like his Father? The fooling and teasing– happy-go-lucky. One thing we can remember is Dad could make

Gram laugh, and we loved seeing that smile and quiet laugh come out. She would just say, "Oh, Allen" because he was always doing or about to do something to get a rise out of someone.

Pictures of Allen

Genevieve

Genevieve at the top of the Empire State Building

Genevieve Larsen was born in 1937 and passed away, way too young, at the age of 43 from pancreatic cancer. I've seen several spellings of her name in my research, so on one visit I asked her daughter Cathy about the proper spelling. Cathy told me her mom changed the spelling after finding out that her father named her after one of his many girlfriends.

Below is a submission from her daughter, Cathy, about memories of her mother and Gram:

Mom was the middle child of what we knew of nine siblings. She may have been the smallest at only five feet tall, and she had a reserved personality. I remember her height because it was generally at an early age when we (her children) were able to say we were taller than her. However, she would remind us that she was still the boss regardless of how big we grew. I think my brothers would agree that she was the disciplinarian of our household. When I look back, I guess I would describe her as small but mighty. She was a strong and determined person, and I admire her for that. She always wanted the best for her children, and had a very strong work ethic.

Above all, her family was most important to her, and she enjoyed spending time with them. I remember weekly family skating nights with Uncle Al's family, weekend camping trips with Uncle Grover's and Uncle Al's families, which would often include long bike rides (at least from my perspective, being rather young).

We always took annual vacations staying in campgrounds and touring different attractions and historic sites around the eastern part of the country.

I remember having strong family ties when we were kids. We frequently visited our aunts and uncles on the weekends. I remember driving around from wherever, when we were out and about, asking which cousins we would be near, and if we could stop and visit. I also remember large Thanksgiving dinners with the Snyder clan, with rows of tables and tons of food. It was then that we would exchange names for Christmas gifts.

She was an Elvis fan. She enjoyed crocheting. She thoroughly enjoyed her grandchildren. When she was battling cancer, she would love reading to Jackie.

I remember surprising her by coming home from school a few days early for Christmas the year that she passed. She was so happy to be able to spend a few extra days with me. I remember helping my dad wrap presents that year because she was taken to the hospital just a few days before Christmas. I was amazed at how she had planned every detail for Christmas, leaving lists of gifts and instructions to be carried out in case she was not there. She tried to plan ahead for the things that she knew she would miss. I was recently engaged at the time, and one of her gifts to me was a set of dishes.

I remember Gram as a soft-spoken, kind and caring person. I remember her raisin cake and rice pudding that she made at Christmas. I enjoyed spending time with her while she lived with us during her recovery from heart surgery. I still remember the poncho she crocheted for me, as she did for my cousins. She crocheted often, making baby blankets and sweaters for grandchildren and great grandchildren.

Genevieve's Wedding

Genevieve, Robert, and Cathy

Genevieve and Robert in Hawaii

Janice

Russell and Janice

Janice was born in 1941. She passed away in 2003 at the age of 62. She had three daughters, but as I understand it, she raised four daughters, with one of them actually being her grand daughter.

Below is a submission from her daughter Ellen on memories of her mother and Gram:

My mom was all about family. She never had much growing up or when she got married to my father Russell. But she would do and go without to help her kids and grandkids. She never had a vacation, but she was always happy. She loved to make dolls for everyone. I was 36 when my mom passed, and not a day goes by that I do not think about her. Not too long after her, my dad passed to go be with her, and that is when my life changed. I know they are looking down on us, but life is not the same. People go and family disappears, but Aunt Dee is always there to help us out. I don't know what more I can say, she was a hard worker, and I wish I had more time with her.

For fun she would go to Atlantic City with her sister Dee one or two times a year. We all would just sit on the porch together. Like I said, not a lot of money. She and my dad liked to watch the Eagles play.

Gram was a sweet person. I would always stop in when I went to Frenchtown skating rink. Thanksgiving she would make apple pie. I hated peeling, but they were good. My mom worked at Trans Teck. She made parts for the Army. After that she worked at K-mart unloading the trucks. Gram never had money, but she always found a way to get something small for every one. The last movie we shot was my son's first birthday, and Gram held him. She passed away shortly after that. Mom loved her family very much, and I know in my heart she sees you, and watches over us.

Jean, Me, Ellen, and Delores

Kenneth

Kenneth was born July 1944. He had a very short life passing away on October 1944. One recounting of his death was that the family was living in Flemington at that time. They were under quarantine, and he was sick. My mother told this story long ago to my niece MaryAnna.

Joy did a little research about the 1940s and found that during 1943 through 1944, the influenza bug was a full-blown epidemic. Many lives were lost because of the spread of this virulent condition. It is believed that this was not caused by a new strain of influenza, but rather a further outbreak of a strain seen many years before.

Kenneth is buried with my mom in the Quaker cemetery.

Discovering Ancestry

English and Dutch

Being adopted, there was never any family history that I knew of, other than my parents' Eastern European Jewish background, which was not a true background for me. After finding my birth family and determining some of my family medical history, the next thing I focused on was ancestry.

Joy and I have watched the television show produced by Lisa Kudrow called, "Who Do You Think You Are?" since its inception. The show takes famous people and helps them find interesting facts and ties to history. As examples, Lisa Kudrow found ties to the Holocaust, Brooke Shields found ties to French royalty, Valarie Bertinelli found ties to William The Conqueror, and Josh Groban found a relative with a musical background.

Now it was my turn to do some digging into the past. While I have yet to search on my father's Dutch side beyond my great grandfather, we have traced my birth mother's side. Like the show, I was amazed to find several historical connections in my family background.

Historical Connections ~ Carver and Doan in my Blood

The most significant find with ties to history came from a direct line from my maternal grandfather, Robert W. Carver. There are two accounts of family ancestry and both have historical significance.

The first account, which I don't believe is true, as it is undocumented and has several gaps in time, traces back ten generations to a supposed eleven times grandfather, James Carver (1527-1568) from Doncaster, Yorkshire, England. He had three sons: Robert Carver, Isaac Carver and John Carver.

This account has his son, Robert Carver, as my ten times grandfather. He came over to the Colonies in the 1620's. As the story goes, he was on a ship with a John Wannamaker, a direct ancestor of the Wannamaker clothier stores.

Robert's brother, John, had a much different place in history. John was a passenger on the Mayflower. John was elected Governor of the ship for the crossing. That Governorship continued when the ship landed in Plymouth, and he was actually the first governor of Plymouth from 1620 until 1621 when he died.

The other account of my family history leads back to a William Carver, who would be my seven times grandfather. This is the family ancestry that I believe to be true, as a result of a document Joy uncovered. The document she found was titled, "Genealogy of William Carver from Hertfordshire, England, in 1682."

Adoption – Changing One's Stars

This account was put together by Elias Carver, an attorney from Doylestown, PA and was published in 1903. This account lists every generation from William Carver's arrival in 1682, all the way to my grandfather Robert W Carver. Giving it authenticity are all the references, with the locations in Friends (also called Quakers) Minute Books and official government records for all births, marriages, deaths, and wills in the family.

Using this account, my seven times grandfather, William, is believed to be the first Carver in my family ancestry to come over from England in 1682. He was born in 1662 in Hertfordshire, England. He came over to the colonies in the same group of ships as William Penn, founder of the Province of Pennsylvania. Penn travelling on the ship "Welcome," and William Carver travelling on the ship "Samson."

They were all part of the religious Society of Friends and settled in the Byberry area of Philadelphia. According to this account, they settled on a tract of land, and dug a cave to live in, until they could build homes.

William Carver married Joan Kinsley in 1689. They had six children, one of whom was my six times grandfather, William, who was born in 1694. It was this William, who married Elizabeth Walmsley in 1719. She was the daughter of parents who were on the ship "Welcome," with William Penn. They gave the couple 244 acres of land in Bucks County. William and Elizabeth settled that land, and they were the first Carvers to live in Bucks County, PA.

They had a son, whom they also named William, who was born in 1721. He married Sarah Strickland in 1755. They had a son, again named William, born in 1756. That William married Phoebe Worthington in 1783. They had a son named Joseph (finally a different name), born in 1788. Joseph married Rebecca White in

1818. They had a son named Eli W., born in 1821. Eli married Hannah Ann Townsend, and they had a son named Robert W., born in 1873. Robert married Louisa Doan. They had a daughter named Elizabeth R., born in 1915, my mother.

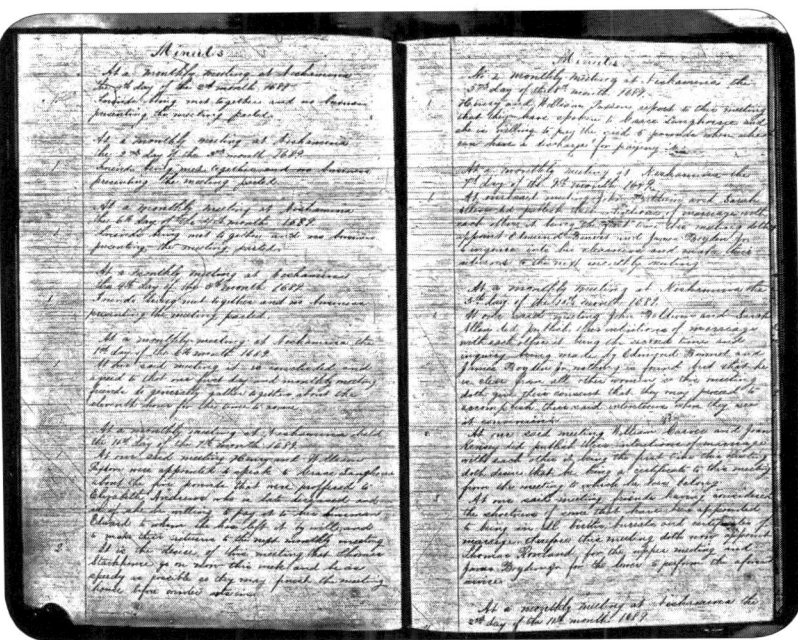

Copy of U.S. Quaker Meeting, Bucks County, Pennsylvania, Middletown Monthly Meeting Minutes. "At a monthly meeting on the 5th day of the 10th month of 1689... At our said meeting William Carver and Joan Kinsley did publish their intentions of marriage with each other, it being the first time this meeting both desire that he bring a certificate to the meeting to which he does belong."

Carversville Postmaster

The next historical connection is to a town in Pennsylvania named Carversville. This town was named after the first and well-liked postmaster, whose last name was Carver, in the year 1833. Since we can trace back our ancestry to the first Carvers in Bucks County, where Carversville is located, I assume somewhere in the ancestral tree is a connection to the postmaster.

The Doan Gang

The last significant historical figure comes from my mother's, mother, Louisa Doan. While we don't yet know if there is a direct ancestral tie, at least her name is tied to the "infamous" Doan Brothers.

This summary contains excerpts from an article by Peter Mulcahy, "The Doan Outlaws of Bucks County, The Life and Times of the Plumstead Cowboys."

The Doan family first came to America in 1629 in Cape Cod, Massachusetts. By 1696, the Doans had moved to Bucks County, Pennsylvania near Plumsteadville. Joseph Doan Sr. and his wife, Hester, fathered five of the six Doan outlaws (Joseph Jr, Moses, Aaron, Levi and Marlon). The sixth was Abraham, who was a first cousin.

They were all handsome and very athletic, be it wrestling, running or jumping. In the Revolutionary War, Moses told the others that since their parents paid no taxes as Quakers, they would lose their property. He convinced the other brothers to fight with the British against the Colonists.

In addition to fighting for the British, the gang also robbed and stole horses. Working regularly for the British as spies and "horse suppliers," their disguises and knowledge of the area let them stay close to the Colonist encampments and pass information on troop movements. Their reports to General Howe on troop movements were so precise, Howe named them "Eagle Spy." The defeat of Washington's Army on Long Island was directly attributed to Moses Doan, who discovered an unprotected backway to the Colonist encampment, and this sent Washington retreating through New Jersey and into Pennsylvania.

Moses Doan was also at Washington's crossing and heard and saw the barges pushing through the blizzard towards the Jersey side. Having in his possession one of the greatest secrets of the war, he tried to warn Colonel Rahl, who ignored the note he was given with Moses Doan's information. Had he read the note, maybe Washington would not have crossed the Delaware River, and who knows where we would be as a country today.

Moses Doan was killed in August 1783. He was buried in a field behind the Village of Fisherville in an unmarked grave, that has never been found.

Abraham and Levi were arrested in Chester County and hung. Their bodies were returned home to Plumstead, where their mother petitioned the Friends to allow them to be buried in the Meeting House Cemetery. The Friends refused, and the cousins' graves can be still seen outside the far left, back wall of the cemetery, located on Ferry Road, just past the Gardenville Inn.

To understand the Friends refusal of the cousins burial, one must understand Quaker beliefs. Since Quakers (or Friends as they refer to themselves), refuse to participate in war, the fact that the Doan Gang participated in the Revolutionary War, barred them from being Quakers and thus barred them from being buried inside a Quaker cemetery.

Reflecting on Roots

I've now gone from no roots to finding my birth family with ties to both the American Revolutionary War (on the wrong side) and either the Pilgrims or most likely the "Welcome Ships" and William Penn, the founder of Pennsylvania. This experience has been similar to those I've watched in the "Who Do You Think You Are?" TV show. Totally unbelievable...and cool historical ties!!

I intend to continue to search farther back and into my father's Dutch ancestry.

Unmasking of Me

Final Accounting

As I write the final chapter, I have to say that through the present time, life's journey for me has been very blessed.

At the onset, being put up for adoption and then being adopted by Lenny and Edith Stamm, were both in, and of themselves, unbelievable changes in fate. Obviously, life would have been so so different if those two events had not taken place. As I said earlier, it changed my stars.

I have my adopted parents to thank for giving me a wonderful childhood, never having to worry about food to eat or a roof over my head. They also afforded me the opportunity of an education. With that opportunity came the ability to forge a fulfilling career with commensurate monetary rewards.

While I was afforded those opportunities, I never took anything for granted, and I worked hard for all the successes, and even harder at the few failures—always taking something away from each experience. Through it all, I was always unwavering in my core values of integrity and work ethic.

I sometimes had wondered where I got my values from, since my adopted father and I were so far apart on how we went about our lives. Only now has it become quite apparent to me, hearing stories of my birth mom and how hard she fought to keep her family together and her work ethic, that I understand where I get my values from. Not only do I owe her my life, for bringing me into this world, but my values and work ethic, as well. I wish I could have met her.

At times, my relationship with my adopted dad has impacted my confidence, and to this day I still sometimes struggle with feelings of inadequacy, in spite of all that I have accomplished. Even though we didn't always agree and had different philosophies about how to live life, in the end, I believe, he loved me and was proud of my accomplishments. My adopted mom throughout all the years was nothing but supportive and loving. Together they made me comfortable in my own skin and in my life, so that I really never felt the need to look for my birth parents. I knew who I was, and who my parents were.

Today, my adopted brother and I have a unique bond that holds us together like never before. We were so different growing up, but now we really are not so different. As long as there is breath in me, I will be there for him. This search and finding my biological siblings changes nothing between him and me—he is my brother.

I've made mistakes along the way just like all of us. Going back I'd only change a couple of things. First, I'd stay fit and secondly, I'd make a bigger effort to live within my means. That said, Joy and I have traveled, alone and with our children, and that provided us great experiences and memories. We also forged relationships with people that we never would have met. So while doing all these things came at a financial price and has somewhat slowed our financial journey to retirement, it was well worth it. Looking back, it's all the memories that are meaningful, and time spent with family—material things really mean nothing.

My family is what it's all about. Joy is my rock. She is there for me, no matter what. Lord knows why, since I'm a little difficult to deal with and can be somewhat moody at times. My kids say that I make faces. I try not to, but I know I do, as I wear my emotions on my sleeve all the time. I'm definitely not a good poker player.

Career has always been second to family. That said, I've developed many lasting relationships at work. I have worked with and led many wonderful people. I've always selected staff that were smarter than me and from diverse backgrounds, so that they all brought something different to the table. Using that formula, I've formed and worked with many great teams.

I believe I've been a good leader and mentor over my career, and that there are many current and future leaders in the company that I have left an impact on. If what I believe is true, I will have left a permanent mark at FPL. I would also hope my legacy would be, "he was a good communicator, a good developer of talent, a people person...a truly good guy." I couldn't ask for more.

Finding my birth family has been nothing short of spectacular. They have been welcoming, accepting and generous. I could never in my wildest dreams have thought of finding such good people.

It was a long journey to get to the point of searching–56 years. It was also a short journey, only a few months to find my birth family, and then only a few short weeks to meet them. Over the past three years we've met a number of times, and I've loved the time we spent together, meeting more and more of my new extended family.

I believe I've developed a good relationship with my remaining siblings. I enjoy talking with my sister, Ruth, and with my brother Leroy. I've also enjoyed sitting on Amos' porch talking to him and Delores about anything and everything.

I've also developed relationships with new nieces and nephews, including those of siblings that have already passed away. It has simply been a remarkable experience.

My cousin, Barbara, asked me when I first met my birth family if I felt a connection with them. At first the answer was, "not really." However, as time has passed and the more we meet and talk, there is definitely a connection building. It's getting stronger everyday.

Sometime soon I need to travel to Kentucky to meet my brother Orville's (Charlie's) wife and daughters. I'm even hopeful that my brother Grover's sons will want to meet as well. Maybe one summer we will arrange a Snyder family reunion, where I could meet even more of my relatives—although there will definitely need to be name tags.

To those of you who are adoptees and are thinking about searching for your birth family, I say, **Just Do It.** You never know what surprises the experience will bring. Even though my experience was a positive one, you also need to be mentally and emotionally prepared for whatever is the outcome of your search—whether it is positive or negative, acceptance or rejection.

I'm also reminded of something my father-in-law said to me during one of his last days on this earth. He said, "Blink, and it's over." I really took that to heart. Life is too short, so don't wait too long to do the things you really want to do. Since he imparted that wisdom to me, I've tried to live and enjoy every day, whatever that day brings.

Stamm Family – October 2014
Front Row: Jordan Dumas, Jeff Stamm, and John Thomas Falkowski. Second Row: Sol Stamm, Joy Stamm, Melissa Falkowski, and John Falkowski. Back Row: Corey Dumas and Sarah Dumas

Epilogue

In Memory of Ruth

My sister Ruth passed away on January 30, 2016. She was my entry into the Synder family, and what an entry it was. From our very first conversation she was completely accepting of me. I will forever remember how she called me **her brother** and told me that she loved me, even though she didn't know me at all.

I recounted that statement to Holly, one of her many grandchildren at her funeral/ celebration of her life, and she corrected me. Holly said, "She has known of you, thought of you, and prayed for you her whole life, so while you only knew of her for the past three years, she has known you your whole life."

I am so thankful for the time I got to spend with her, getting insight into her life, the family, and my mom. I can still see her talking to me from her chair in her family room. I will always remember and cherish the time we spent together.

Ruth,
Rest in peace,
Your brother

Reference To Help With Adoption Search

OmniTrace
www.omnitrace.com
888-965-6696

Florida Adoption Reunion Registry (FARR)
1317 Winnewood Boulevard
Tallahassee, FL 32399
800-96-ADOPT

International Soundex Reunion Registry
www.ISRR.org

Florida Department of Children and Families
www.myflorida.com
1317 Winnewood Boulevard
Tallahassee, FL 32399

Adoption Medical History Registry
Hillcrest, 2nd Floor
PO Box 2675
Harrisburg, PA 17105

PA Department of Health
Division of Vital Records
PO Box 1528
New Castle, PA 16103

First Judicial District of Pennsylvania
Court of Common Pleas
Family Division
1801 Vine Street
Adoption Branch, Room 332
Philadelphia, PA 19103
(215) 686-4194

Appendix

Lists

I don't know if it is a little of the OCD in me or something that I picked up from my adoptive father, who used to do math problems in his head to keep his mind sharp, but I keep lists in my head of things that have happened during my life. My wife is amazed at how I remember things and places we have been to with great detail. I am also good at remembering names and lyrics of songs, as well as who the artist is. Here are a couple of lists from my memory of cruises taken and concerts attended.

Ship	Line	Date	Location	Length
Mardi Gras	Carnival	1977	Caribbean	7
Leonardo Di Vinci	Costa	1978	Caribbean	5
Southward	NCL	1979	Caribbean	7
Festival	Carnival	1980	Caribbean	7
Sunward II	NCL	1981	Caribbean	3
Emerald Seas	Eastern	1981	Caribbean	4
Holiday	Carnival	1987	Caribbean	7
Oceanic (Big Red Boat)	Premiere	1990	Caribbean	5
Holiday	Carnival	1995	Caribbean	7
Destiny	Carnival	1999	Caribbean	7
Norwegian SKY	NCL	2000	Alaska	7
Norwegian Majesty	NCL	2001	New England	7
Carnival Legion	Carnival	2002	Central America	9
Navigator of the Seas	Royal	2003	Caribbean	7
Queen Mary II	Cunard	2004	New York/Caribbean	10

Sovereign of the Seas	Royal	2005	Caribbean	4
Splendor of the Seas	Royal	2005	Mediterranean	7
Jewel of the Seas	Royal	2005	Caribbean	12
Jewel of the Seas	Royal	2006	Baltics	12
Caribbean Princess	Princess	2006	Caribbean	7
Jewel of the Seas	Royal	2007	British Isles/Norway	7
Emerald Princess	Princess	2007	Caribbean	10
Costa Fortuna	Costa	2007	Caribbean	7
Emerald Princess	Princess	2008	Caribbean	10
Sovereign of the Seas	Royal	2008	Caribbean	4
Splendor of the Seas	Royal	2009	Adriatic	7
Emerald Princess	Princess	2009	Caribbean	10
Diamond Princess	Princess	2009	Alaska	14
Navigator of the Seas	Royal	2009	Caribbean	4
Equinox	Celebrity	2010	Caribbean	10
Norwegian SKY	NCL	2010	Caribbean	4
Oasis of the Seas	Royal	2011	Caribbean	7
Destiny	Carnival	2011	Caribbean	4
Allure of the Seas	Royal	2012	Caribbean	7
Millennium	Celebrity	2012	Caribbean	4
Constellation	Celebrity	2013	Transatlantic	16
Reflection	Celebrity	2013	Caribbean	7
Constellation	Celebrity	2013	Caribbean	4
Equinox	Celebrity	2014	Mediterranean	14
Getaway	NCL	2014	Caribbean	7
Freedom of the Seas	Royal	2014	Caribbean	4
Equinox	Celebrity	2015	Transatlantic	16
Reflection	Celebrity	2015	Caribbean	7
Constellation	Celebrity	2015	Caribbean	4

As of December 31, 2015 – 44 cruises – 329 days at sea

Freedom	Carnival	2016	Carribean	4
Solstice	Celebrity	2016	Australia/New Zealand	13

346 days at sea

Appendix

Concerts Attended

4 Tops	Jethrow Tull
5th Dimension	Jimmy Buffett
Adele	KC & The Sushine Band
Allman Brothers	Kelly Clarkson
Aretha Franklin	Linkin Park
B52s	Lovin Spoonful
Barbara Streisand	Maroon 5
Barry Manilow	Matchbox Twenty
Beach Boys	Michael Jackson
BeeGees	Michael McDonald
Bette Midler	Neil Diamond
Billy Joel	Neil Sedaka
Carol King	New Found Glory
Chicago	Night Rangers
Cold Play	NSYNC
Cornelius Brothers and Sister Rose	Paul McCartney
Daughtry	Seals & Crofts
Donna Summers	Steely Dan
Doobie Brothers	Stone Temple Pilots
Earth, Wind & Fire	Supremes
Elton John	Tavares
Eric Clapton	Temptations
Fleetwood Mac	Tom Jones
Goo Goo Dolls	Tommy James
Good Charlotte	Tony Bennett
Hall & Oats	Village People
Hoobastank	Wayne Newton
James Taylor	Wings
Jefferson Airplane	Yes

Favorite Bands, Not Seen in Concert

America   Beatles

Made in the USA
Middletown, DE
05 September 2022